W9-ANG-251

MISSION CRITICAL
A VETERAN'S TOUR OF DUTY
IN PUBLIC EDUCATION
ERIC A. COMBS

© 2014 by Eric A. Combs. All rights reserved.

No part of this document may be reproduced or transmitted in any form or by any means, electronic, mechanical, photocopying, recording, or otherwise, without prior written permission of the author, with the exception of brief excerpts for inclusion in scholarly works or inclusion in reviews. For permissions or further information, post Potemkin Media Omnibus, Ltd. at 140 E. Broadway Ave., Tipp City, O. 45371.

Copy Editor: Kate Johnsen; Cover Design: Stephen Dale Marlowe; Cover Drafting & Design: Austin Labig

Combs, Eric A.

Mission Critical / by Eric A. Combs 278 pp. 1.48 cm.

ISBN-13 978-1-940876-06-1

Foxhead Books

ACKNOWLEDGEMENTS

Above all, I must recognize my wife Elizabeth, without whom I would have never amounted to much. She has been my confidante, friend, and advisor, and is truly the best person I have ever known.

To the men and women in the US Armed Forces I have worked with, and those who still work for our freedom today. Having been "raised" in the Air Force, I learned a good many things about leadership, honor, and selflessness.

Also, I couldn't have done this work without the experiences and expertise of Team Delta (Suzanne Bell, Betsy Wyatt, Betsy Chadd, Ann Beeman, and Matt Ehlinger). What a great team of teachers. I am indebted to them for any successes I may have had in the classroom. Lastly, thanks to Major Anthony Rulli, who was the person that started me on this journey in education.

CONTENTS

Introduction

April 20, 1999, was a long day. All days are long in Korea, I've found, but this was the longest.

I was in the Air Force and assigned as the Chief of Air Base Defense at Osan Air Base, an American base in South Korea. We were only a few miles from the demilitarized zone, the swath of land separating North and South, in a country still technically at war.

I was serving a short tour without my family, so other than work, what was there to do? I tossed my keys on the counter of my barracks room, dropped my rucksack, and started to relax. While I missed my family terribly, it was a good assignment with hard-working people, well-trained troops, and a serious mission at the front of our minds: protect the Korean Peninsula.

I was a Senior Master Sergeant at the time, and worked with a young Captain who had recently arrived from the Air Force

Academy. Our office ensured all of the combat operations plans for the protection of the base were maintained, updated, and ready to go at a minute's notice. In our second role, we were the operational controlling element for all defensive forces for the base. We coordinated and trained with the South Korean Special Forces as well as our own Special Operation units. We were well trained and ready for anything; we could, within minutes if required, bring to bear a considerable amount of firepower to any target that may threaten our base.

On that day, however, I had never felt so vulnerable and weak in all my life.

The computer was on, and I was checking messages from my wife when I saw the words "Columbine, Colorado" appear in the headlines. I remember staring at the computer screen in my barracks, stunned at the atrocity, helpless, completely unable to do anything about it. I had at my disposal enough trained men, deadly weapons, and high-tech military equipment to fend off a major offensive from another nation—or to take the fight to them, if necessary. I had these things at my beck and call. And yet, kids were killing kids back home, and I could do nothing about it. Have you ever sat for an hour, not moving, because you were too stunned to even think?

The media blitz afterward was incredible. It was hard to know what to believe. Everyone in the media and elsewhere were quick to try and assign blame, to find something that might make sense of this horror story of students killing their classmates and teachers. Reports suggested that the attacks occurred because the students were teased, or because they were loners. They were playing violent video games and belonged to a supposed "trench-coat gang." We heard these theories and a dozen more from the media or the talking heads they trotted out to fill airtime and "cover" the tragedy. And many people seemed to believe these theories—it was almost as if they wanted to come up with a "reason" for this horrible massacre.

So many deaths, so much pain. And while I may have tried to dedicate a good part of my life to serving my country, I realized that my commitment was overshadowed by an enemy within.

In those first dark hours, I thought seriously about what I could do to help, if anything. I had 19 years in the Air Force and was privileged to work with some of our nation's very best people, but I could not shake the feeling that we needed to reexamine our country and ourselves. Where was the value and concern for our education system? Since when did kids start killing kids? It seemed as if something was broken in the country I served, something deep and meaningful and, unfortunately, permanent.

Of course, this wasn't the first attack within our schools, and it hasn't been the last. The American psyche has changed over the past decades, and the sacred vow to protect the defenseless no longer carries the strength and ability it once may have had. It was for this reason I decided to become a teacher. I loved learning and loved history, so I figured it was a good match.

And while I did well in the field of education, my journey was far different than I could have imagined.

Into the Blue

To start, it would probably be prudent to give you a little bit of background information about myself. Not with hubris, mind you, but rather as an opportunity for you to gain a little perspective to better understand my point of view. Believe me, the only reason this background information is even remotely important is so that you can better judge why I behave the way I do—and say the things that I do.

Arizona

I was raised in Surprise, Arizona, a tiny suburb northwest of Phoenix. My father and mother were divorced by the time I was nine years old. My two brothers and I spent many hours wandering the Sonoran desert landscape northwest of Phoenix and would spend days out in the gullies and dry riverbeds, creating forts, jumping our bikes, and chasing each other in games of tag, tackle, or super heroes.

My father remarried, and our clan of boys increased by two as we moved to west Phoenix. We immediately got along as a small tribe of boys, and the pecking order was determined in a lot of wrestling matches and exploration that often resulted in bloody noses and broken household items. We would fight a lot, but not out of anger. We were just being boys. We would always stick up for one another when an outsider tried to pick on one of our brothers!

As the oldest of now five boys, I was the built-in babysitter. At an early age, I completely understood what "the buck stops here" meant—that I was in charge completely. As the oldest, and babysitter, I had all the responsibility but no authority. If something happened on my watch, it was always my fault. Needless to say, this quickly got old. By the time I was 17, and after years and years of being responsible for my brothers, I was very ready to move on to the real world.

I did very well in school, even if I was extremely bored, but due to our family's financial situation, college was never really an option for me or any of my brothers. In fact, the concept of going to college was never mentioned one time in our home. And when my father was laid off from a government contract job after 19 years, things got really tense at the Combs' household.

One of my high school teachers talked to me about college and my options, but the guidance counselors all reminded me only about the courses I would need to take to graduate, ignoring any classes I might need to do to qualify for higher learning. Everyone understood that college just wasn't in the cards for any of us.

My brothers all went to very different careers: one followed in my father's mechanical steps by becoming an automobile mechanic, one became a preacher, one is a draftsman/designer, and the youngest brother manages a system of warehouses for a large company.

One day, my prospects changed abruptly. A sharply dressed Marine came to our high school and spoke eloquently about things that really mattered to me, things like honor, country, and duty. As I listened to him talk, I could only think of getting out, of escaping my Arizona home. Like I said, I had great grades but the diploma didn't have any real meaning for me at the time. I had worked from the age of 14 and had my first car at 15, so I figured I could do anything I put my mind to. After hearing the Marine, I decided that this was my next step, my first one out into the world. I took the Armed Services Vocational Aptitude Battery (ASVAB) and scored well, well enough, in fact, to have my pick of jobs.

The only hurdle was Dad.

Since I was 17 and had not yet completed high school, I needed two things to qualify for the Armed Forces: I needed to take the GED and get a parent's permission to join the military. Dad was prior Air Force and, for some bizarre reason, was reluctant to let me scoot off to the infantry or some force reconnaissance unit. My father held the odd notion that I was destined to fix things like him. He also knew I was foolhardy enough to volunteer for just about anything. He really felt I could eventually learn to fix things and get a trade like he did. Hardly! I think his reasoning was that I could get a respectable job using the "family gift" of mechanical intelligence. Sadly, I'm completely lacking in that department.

He wouldn't sign for me to join the Army or Marines. It wasn't even an option. But he relented on the concept of joining the military if, and only if, I signed up with the Navy or Air Force. As I was not fond of water at the time, and being raised in the desert didn't really give me a lot of opportunity to become a strong swimmer, I reluctantly made my way to the Air Force recruiter's office.

My first challenge was finding a career path that sounded interesting. The litany of choices, listed in a huge three-ring binder, was incredible. I suddenly had so many options: aircraft maintenance, electronics, nuclear weapons, and dozens more. I quickly bypassed aircraft mechanic, fuels specialist, and aerospace ground equipment, as they all sounded like the one thing I hated: fixing things. Dad would have loved them, but I had never been good at it, and I never would be.

But when the Staff Sergeant mentioned the words "grenade launcher" and "M-60 machine gun," I perked right up. He said it was a special division of the Air Force Security Police field known as Air Base Ground Defense (ABGD), and I suddenly knew exactly what I wanted to do: train to become a military policeman first, and then volunteer for ABGD duty.

I joined to be a security policeman, a career field that would later became known as Security Forces. In doing so, I probably saved many lives—not by protecting them from harm, mind you. I mean that I have no aptitude with tools and have no business working on any machine.

It turned out that ABGD was a subgroup under the police, and while there were plans to separate it at the time, it stayed as the combat component of the police function. This was an important distinction because throughout my career I gravitated toward that component of the career field rather than police or security duty.

I signed up, and since Dad signed the papers at home, he did not know about what career field I had chosen. I left for boot camp the very next day. To his surprise, I came home eight months later wearing a Security Forces beret. And a smirk.

Basic

I'm a short man; some would say an extremely short man. I personally think most people are just overly tall. It's been something I've had to deal with my entire life, a fact that became abundantly clear to me when I got off the bus at Lackland Air Force Base to start my basic training.

I will never forget my reception. The training instructor (TI) strode up to me quickly as I climbed off the bus, clicking his metal heels together loudly and yelling, "Get in line, get in line! You people make me sick! Line up by height right now!" It was then that I knew life was about to get a bit more challenging.

Apparently, all of the rest of the recruits were prior basketball stars. I was easily a foot shorter than the next man in the lineup. The TI clicked down the line, yelling at each of the men in turn, then stopped dead in front of me.

"Where's the rest of you?" he screamed.

Now, I knew they are going to give me a rough time, but I wasn't expecting this.

"Open your bag!" he screamed at me. "Open it!" A second

later, my bag of belongings was unceremoniously flung to the concrete. "Get back on the bus! Find the rest of you!"

I suddenly found myself scrambling back up the steps onto the bus, looking under the seats for the "rest" of me. All the while, a five-striped madman screamed at me from outside the bus. "Look under the bus! I can't take half a man!" The TI yelled, much to his pleasure. "Why didn't you join the Army?"

Then it came, the name that would follow me for the next few years.

"Point five! Get back here, line up," he yelled. "Looks like the Air Force gets screwed again!"

Welcome to the United States Air Force.

The nickname stuck for a while. Some of my friends would say I've tried the rest of my life to erase that nickname of "half a man."

I got through those early days of basic training, though, and managed to keep my head down. I made honor graduate at the US Air Force Security Police Academy, then won the Top Gun award for both rifle and machine gun. I did equally well in Air Base Defense School and heavy weapons training, which were both run by the Army at the time. I loved conducting combat patrols and had a naturally ability with land navigation.

Ironically, I joined to escape the harsh Arizona desert—and my very first duty assignment was at Luke Air Force Base, located in beautiful Glendale, Arizona, approximately 20 miles from my home. My goal of seeing the world had gotten off to a very lackluster start—I could practically see my boyhood home from the base.

During the course of my career in the US Air Force, I was fortunate to work with some of the most elite military teams in the world. I trained on nuclear recapture missions, joined and eventually trained SWAT teams, British Army and Air Force Special Operations teams, and did a fair amount of rappelling, fast roping, explosive entry (also known as breaching), and tactical operations.

I served nine years overseas altogether, finding myself in Egypt, Kuwait, Saudi Arabia, Germany, England, and South Korea, among other places. And during those times, I earned two more nicknames, more accurately known as call signs: "Madhobbit" and "Shrike." I will detail how I earned both of these call signs later. To this day, I am still known by a few by those sacred labels, names that I'm proud to carry because, unlike "half a man," these call signs were earned on the field of battle.

If it weren't for the Air Force, I don't know what would have happened to me. They provided a professional education, training, and a home. I learned teamwork and trust, and saw most of the planet. It took six years and three associate's degrees for me to finish a bachelor's degree. Why? I moved every few years and most universities took very few credits from other colleges. I received my B.A. in anthropology from the University of Wyoming through a program called Bootstrap with the Air Force. It was an officer commissioning program that assisted enlisted members to become officers after they have served a certain amount of time and get degrees in specific areas. My dream was to apply for the Central Identification Laboratory as a forensic anthropologist in Hawaii and repatriate war dead from battlefields in Korea and Vietnam.

But soon after I got my degree, Saddam Hussein invaded Kuwait, and that put the lives—and plans—of everyone in the military on hold. After the first Gulf War, there was a huge draw down in the Air Force, and those members of the enlisted ranks who attempted to become officers were put on a very thin scale, meaning that very few applications for officer training were being processed. The ones that were submitted by enlisted members married to enlisted were no longer being accepted. They had a concern that an enlisted member married to an officer could affect the overall effectiveness of both. (I won't share my opinion on that score.) My wife was a staff sergeant in the Air Force and was the driving force behind my entry into the world of higher education. Because of the draw-downs and being married to an enlisted member, my final attempt at becoming an officer was crushed so I pressed on with my enlisted career.

I did well in the Air Force and received quite a few more awards and distinctions along the way. In 1992, I was selected as the top enlisted sergeant for all Air Force members in Europe. I was fortunate to train with and advise British Special Forces and Korean Forces on air defense operations, weaponry, and tactics. The last 10 years of my career I spent training small tactical units on counter-terrorism and hostage rescue operations. I had the honor of working with some fantastic tacticians as team members, many of whom I stay in contact with today.

In my 20th year of service, I returned from South Korea and was looking at a good shot at the top enlisted rank, Chief Master Sergeant. I was stationed at Wright-Patterson Air Force Base, Ohio, after Korea—but the problem was there was no job for me. I had promoted myself out of a position, and the only way I would be able to put on the rank of chief would be to do another remote tour in hopes that a position would open up for me in Ohio, where my wife was stationed. In Ohio, I had finally bought a home and my daughter was in the local high school. My family had spent a lot of holidays, birthdays, and critical events in life without a dad or·husband present. When my daughter found out that I didn't make chief the first time, she was actually quite happy, saying that she got to keep her daddy for another year. The idea of having to leave again, to move on to the next duty station, was too much for me to handle. To honor my daughter's tear-filled eyes, I decided to retire from the Air Force.

It took twenty years for me to learn an important lesson: your character must set your priorities, and character will tell you what the right decision is. In the military practice of land navigation, before the vaunted GPS (Global Positioning Satellite) came along, the very first thing you do is orient your map and compass, to set them pointing in the right direction. Once that was done, you can find any spot on earth within a meter.

But while the setting of the compass (our values) and the orientation of our map (response to our experiences) is not always such an easy task, it's absolutely critical to keep that compass bearing. It is tough to navigate the world when your compass is off and leads you to places you do not want to go or do not belong.

Out

So, I was thirty-eight years old and had absolutely no idea what I wanted to do when I "grew up."

The only inkling I had was perhaps to teach, but while I was enlisted, I dreamed of earning "real money." I believe every enlisted member who retires has this idea that since I served my country, I should be able to serve my family and myself and get the "real" money out there somewhere in the civilian world.

I started ramping up my resume and quickly found out that some words are not very welcomed by civilians. Words like "sniper," "grenade launcher," and "explosive entry," while all very fun endeavors, truly scare the daylights out of most people. "Civilian-izing" my resume wasn't easy for me, but completing twenty years of difficult courses like air base defense operations, air assault, tactical radio operator, and explosive breaching mean absolutely nothing to civilian employers.

Luckily, I was also trained as a facilitator for the Stephen Covey Seven Habits course, Quality Air Force Management, Process Improvement Team Management, four levels of professional military education, and command air base defense school, and these courses were much easier to translate into useful civilian knowledge and skill descriptions that had valid meaning to potential bosses.

When I retired from the Air Force, I really had thought that I finally would be making decent money. No one enters the military for financial gain. I went to the transition classes to learn to present myself during interviews. I bought a single suit and started sending out resumes.

When my retirement was final, I soon accepted a very lucrative job as a production manager in the local Ohio automotive industry. I had received a call from a large company about becoming a line production manager. Finally, I would be starting a career with financial promise, and providing a decent living for my family after such a long time of sacrifice! My rose-colored glasses, filled with visions of honor, duty to country, and service before self, were about to get smacked right off my face.

Industry

Actually, I did well in industry, truth be told. I soon had seventy-seven employees, and in my single year at the plant we broke two local production records. I was selected for the factory council and received laudatory comments from my superiors. The money and perks were both good.

I also loathed every moment in that place.

I simply could not adapt to two major elements in this new life: managers working over people instead of with them, and the idea of individuals working together but not as a team.

I was yelled at by the representatives of the workers' union for helping an employee make a deadline. Conversely, I was told by my management team that it was the union's job to take care of the workers, not mine. Then it hit me—this was not a team.

The problem was I didn't like it; in fact, I really couldn't stomach it. I was making money for the sake of money, and for some bizarre and strange reason, I couldn't see how what I did benefited anyone. When I would offer up help to my employees, I would get "talked" to by either management or the union.

I couldn't seem to learn these strange new rules of "teamwork." In my experience, the best commanders were the ones that got in there and did the work with you, showing that they knew the process and respected what each person did. I learned from people who weren't afraid to get their hands dirty, and from those examples, I learned respect for the chain of command.

I remember General Dieker in Korea—when he spoke to the command staff, I always had the sense that he knew exactly what our jobs were and how they were best done. I figured that, somewhere along the line, he'd done all of our jobs, and probably had done a better job at them. He was also an F-16 pilot, and was always ready to launch his bird during exercises, fighting alongside the rest of us.

This new concept of detached leadership baffled me. I had real difficulty thinking that I was expected look down on my fellow teammate, especially when they could use a hand, and not do anything to help. No matter how hard life was in the military, I could always guarantee two things: I was making a difference in the world, and my brother or sister in arms was there for me. They had my back, and I had theirs. Whether I was training a tactical team or creating plans to defend an air base, I could always see where my labor would help, usually using it to protect others from harm. As cheesy as that might sound, this resolve was buried deep in me and has always helped me remember how important teamwork and working for the greater good truly can be.

At the automotive facility, there was a fifty-year-old woman assigned to working with some of the hardest and heaviest automobile parts. She was new to the company and was taking care of her granddaughter while her daughter finished drug rehab. But she couldn't keep up with the workload; the work was back-breaking. I could walk through that plant and see plenty of able bodies working much lighter jobs, but those were reserved for something called "seniority." I later learned this term was often used as a legal excuse not to improve oneself.

Well, complaints came down the line that the woman could not keep up with the rest of the assembly line. I tried to get her reassigned to a job she could physically do, you know, to keep a motivated and valued member of the team in the game. No go. I was told to terminate her from the position, which I did. Management gave me kudos for being able to walk her out of the factory, as if firing someone from a job was some kind of accomplishment. She even thanked me for being kind and understood why I had to do what I did. Management also told me that I was shaping up to be great supervisor material.

That night, I threw up and couldn't sleep. I felt that it wasn't right to ruin a person's life in the name of production. I believe in capitalism and open markets, but I also believe that a nation, town, or organization without a soul is one that need not be served. I had to find another way.

So, with my inability to reconcile this situation in my heart, I started searching for something more meaningful, a place where I could make a difference.

It was then I realized that all the training from the Air Force might have become a hindrance to me. Training tactical teams (combat patrols, SWAT teams, etc.) was not applicable to a lot of jobs out there. While I can personally tell you that a senior NCO in the military can do almost anything, it's rather tough to convince others on the outside. For example, while I was in the Air Force, I received Quality Management Training, Covey Institute Training, Instructional Leadership, Organizational Behavioral Management, training on OSHA Standards, and learned how to create training plans and field units from cradle to operational status. All the training most corporate world managers get, we got. And the standards were higher in military training: in training for the Strategic Air Command, everyone in our unit had to achieve a 90% or better on all job qualifications. If you received an 89% or below, you received remedial training. The expectations were high, and rightly so. When human lives depended on it, you could afford nothing in terms of mistakes.

I found that my efforts to help improve my people's lives were constantly challenged at the factory from both the union and management, and the atmosphere of mistrust was palpable.

On one occasion, I handed out leaflets for a local community college for my employees because the company would pay for college for members in good standing after they had completed their 90 days of probation. I was quickly reminded that it was the union's job to give this information, and my behavior was viewed as being very suspicious. When I tried to explain that a good leader takes care of their troops, the union reminded me that was their job.

Worse still, I saw how we, as an organization, were wasting money and manpower through a set of unrealistic and foolish rules. If I had to get production running on the weekend, I often had to ensure that several other employees, who would not be used in any capacity, would be available for that day and earning double or triple time. If I stepped in to help an employee, they would write me up for doing wage labor.

Often I would still do it because the cost of paying someone else for not doing work was less than the money we made the company by increased production. Even though we had made exceptional numbers and produced high-quality products, I was too constrained by ignorant and petty rules to take my team to a higher performance level. Leading by example was not just a foreign concept here, it was an impossibility. Not only was it not allowed, it was actively discouraged.

When I found myself working in the civilian world, most places had very little understanding of the concepts of working as a team, dedication to the mission and vision, and, most of all, loyalty to their troops. I would repeatedly see managers make simple mistakes while trying to manage people and materials. Often, they allowed fear to rule the workplace or simply gave in to inaction. Letting ego interfere with their jobs was the offense I saw most often. It was always a dangerous proposition, and yet I witnessed account after account of broken teams with broken leaders trying to accomplish something.

Worst of all, I found that working for the almighty dollar was a very hollow existence. I gained weight, broke out in boils, and developed chest pains.

After a year of this, I started looking for a way out, but had little luck. Adjusting my skill set to the civilian world was difficult. For example, my expertise in defending air bases and training tactical teams did not help me much, but I tried to apply it to the civilian world. I applied for hundreds of positions, such as security director for airports, but heard nothing. Hundreds of resumes flew out the door. I came close to landing a security position at a large local museum, but that was about it. I had too much training, too much experience, for most law enforcement or security positions. I did get a call about a position with a company working in Iraq, good money and right up my old alley, but my wife had enough of my traipsing around the world.

Classroom

A phone call with a voice from the past changed everything for me. The man on the phone remembered a tactical demonstration our team had put on for a bunch of Air Force Junior ROTC cadets years earlier. We took them hostage and then used our team to rescue them. In fact, my daughter was among the students, and when we rappelled down from the hangar ceiling to "rescue" them, she beamed with pride as we took down the bad guys. The ROTC kids had loved it, the tactical demonstration team had loved it, and I remember having quite a good time myself.

"How would you like to teach high school?" Major Rulli asked.

My heart jumped and so did I, and I told him so. He got me an interview within a week, and I was hired on the spot.

The first hurdle was the significant cut in pay. I still remember my wife saying, "You're going to be just a teacher?" Telling my wife we'd have a $45,000 "change" in income wasn't the easiest conversation we'd ever had, but she knew the other job was killing me. She, like I, had high hopes of better pay and a better lifestyle based on twenty years of experience in tactical operations, training, and planning. She had seen me through years of deployments, separations, and a few scary moments we still do not talk about. I am blessed to have such a strong woman to advise and love me to this day.

I had to get trained as a JROTC instructor in Alabama, but since the school year was almost ready to start, I had the first year waived. So, three months later, I found myself in front of

35 high school cadets in my first classroom. Apparently, I was grinning from ear to ear. I had found a new home, albeit one with many new challenges.

I remember my new boss, a retired principal who had served in Vietnam. He looked at me and simply said, "I know your kind, crazy snake eaters! Just don't get me thrown in jail, okay?" I said "Yes, sir," and he said "Stop that! My name is 'Bob,' not 'sir'!"

This was my start in public education, but soon I would come face to face with that in which I was not proficient: politics in education.

Currently, funding of public schools in Ohio is a really big problem. Even the state Supreme Court has said so. Our little community was overtaxed and fraught with issues of distrust and misunderstanding. More cuts were coming soon, and reading the tea leaves, I figured I had better make myself more valuable quickly if I wanted to stay employed.

Our principal was toying with the idea of creating a team of teachers to address one of our greatest concerns: ninth graders who are at risk of failing their first year of high school. It was one of those jobs where people would shake your hand and thank you for taking it. You know, a suicide mission.

But I initially had a big problem: no license to teach any subject other than military science. I had a bachelor's in anthropology, but no license for the state.

Thus began my trek to obtain the coveted piece of paper that meant I was legal and qualified to stand in a classroom in front of a bunch of students.

So, You Want to be a Real Teacher?

I initially encountered a few social obstacles upon my entrance to nonmilitary life. The first thing I had to learn was how to become a civilian. In many respects, I had to learn how to respond more humanely to my students than I was used to. The military raises good stoics, men and women who are loyal and effective, yet I felt I lacked some of the more "personable" qualities desired by many.

Dealing with Civilians

When I started teaching, I discovered that there were major differences in this new culture among educators. To begin with, I quickly found out that saying "ma'am" to many middle-aged women is, in fact, not a sign of respect. Several times, I got what I perceived to be "the evil eye" for doing nothing more than trying to be polite. I would hold a door open or respond to a question with a "Yes, ma'am," but sometimes received a baleful look of derision.

I had never before worked in a setting with women in the majority, and it took an astute principal to set me straight. He took me aside and briefed me on why some of the staff were routinely squinting their threatening eyes at me. He told me the women didn't like to be referred to as "ma'am" because they felt I was referring to their age or talking down to them—the same went for holding the door and other actions that I'd always seen as basic politeness.

Not all the ladies reacted this way, to be sure, but a couple of them really did give me pause to consider how to deal with the issue. Some thanked me for being polite, and others just gave me "the look" to let me know they were not happy with my actions or words.

One day, I watched as one of the ladies tried to pull open a door while holding several boxes. I decided then that others would simply have to get used to me. I held open the door for the lady and smiled, completely ignoring her retort, "I have this!"

Another difficulty I faced early on in my career was a more casual atmosphere than I was used to in a workplace environment, especially among the teachers and other staff. For example, first names did not come easy for me. I was used to a much more formal approach, and, to this day, I still find myself struggling with saying a casual "Hi" to Bob, Sally, or Mary. I tend to stay focused at work, and while I can be fairly funny talking to groups or in a casual crowd, at work, I am all business. On many occasions, I have had to let people know that many of my facial expressions are similar. In other words, my intense face, happy face, and frustrated face all pretty much look exactly the same to the uninitiated.

JROTC

Although I was very keen to teach kids, I didn't receive a lot of information about how to do it. I initially started as an Air Force Junior ROTC instructor. Actually, I was already qualified to do that, having a bachelor's degree and more than 15 years in the military. I was then sent to Maxwell Air Force Base, outside of Montgomery, Alabama, to learn how to teach JROTC students.

I should explain that JROTC, or Junior Reserve Officer Training Corps, is a program specifically designed to teach discipline, teamwork, and "esprit de corps" to young people of high school age. A school derives many advantages by having a unit; one of the biggest is that half the instructor's salary is paid by the supporting military service. The courses taught include military science, aerospace science, military and American history, drill and ceremony, and character education.

At my first assignment teaching JROTC, my supervisors were an Air Force Major and a Senior Master Sergeant (SMSgt) who retired from the nuclear medicine career field. Both of these gentlemen gave me my first glimpses into dealing with kids, parents, and the creature known as public education. Admittedly, with the exception of the students, I encountered almost no real surprises in this environment. I was back in uniform, teaching students in uniforms who were mostly volunteers, and I was happy to be serving the students. Everything around me seemed familiar with one exception: the students.

The students were a bit of a challenge when I first arrived, fresh out of training. Now, understand that a classroom of JROTC cadets should be a dream job (and an easy first assignment) for most new teachers. If everything went according to plan, I would walk in, the cadets would stand up sharply, and then I would say, "Seats!" The cadets would rapidly sit down and prepare to take notes. Oh the joy!

And while 98% of JROTC cadets are fully compliant and are easy to mold, that 2% can kill you, every time. A few students end up in JROTC because frustrated parents want them to be "fixed." They have the opinion that a little discipline and stern instruction would do them good. While I do not disagree that discipline can help anyone, the reason for submitting to it needs to be clear in both the parent's and child's minds. No one wakes up in the morning thinking, "I would love to lock down a few kids before lunch!" ("Locking down" means to stand toe to toe and screaming in their faces.) This is often the picture these parents would have of JROTC instructors. In all actuality, we operate under the same rules as the other teachers, except perhaps we could be a bit more stringent, somewhat like a coach can be for their team. So, when some of these kids arrive, they are automatically a disruption in the classroom, or at least that's what they try to be.

Dealing with Emotional Outbursts

When I left the JROTC classroom, moving on to teach at-risk ninth grade (Delta) students, I noticed a distinct shift in behaviors and attitudes. Some people have told me they would not have been able to deal with the "Delta" kids, but I truly enjoyed working with them. Some had an edge to them, a chip that sometimes needed to be flicked off the shoulder, while others were very withdrawn and quiet. The greatest thing about these kids was that they all needed us—some quite desperately.

I soon realized that my education in being a real teacher had just begun, and begun in earnest. The first challenge of teaching the at-risk ninth grade students was understanding that, for some strange reason, not all students were in my classroom to learn. I know, that's probably next to impossible to believe, but some of my charges weren't interested in learning new things. Not in the least. Crazy, huh?

My first approach was, of course, a military one. In my mind, these students simply needed to be briefed and, through my extensive sergeant's wisdom, then their intrinsic motivation will kick in. Soon they'll be learning and motivated and racing their way up Maslow's hierarchy of needs! Right?

Not.

One girl came into the classroom wailing to beat the band. For you northern folks, "to beat the band" means she was crying. A lot. Her sobbing sounded as if she had just found out she had contracted some kind of major fatal disease, one that would bring about a catastrophic and earth-shattering life change.

I sat her down and tried to calm her, my training instantly kicking in. Panic has never helped anyone, outside of the Hitchhiker's Guide to the Galaxy books.

I looked her square in the eyes, giving her a reassuring look that let her know I was in command of my feelings and was there to help. "Hon, I need to know how to help you," I said, "so take a deep cleansing breathe and calm down."

Her bottom lip continued to quiver and the tears never really stopped. After a minute, she could at least begin to form basic sentences. I guided her through a few cleansing breaths. Here it comes. Soon, I thought, I would be able to fix this kid, help her deal with the life-changing trauma she was facing, and then we could all be back on the fast track to "learning town."

"Mmm, ma... my.... boyfriend... broke..... up with me!" The last three words were slammed together as they rushed out of her mouth. A new torrent of tears and sobbing began.

My wisdom and North American maleness immediately jumped into action.

"Is that all?" I asked, incredulous. "Why, you're crying over nothing. You'll get another one in no time. Just think: now, you have more time to focus on your schoolwork!"

It all sounded very logical—and reasonable—to me. Thinking back on it, I get the feeling that I probably sounded more like Boris Karloff as the Grinch to her, trying to convince Little Cindy Loo Who to go back to bed while I steal the Christmas tree! All of the other teachers were probably wondering, how did this dolt get into a classroom?

The young woman gave me one of those how-could-you? looks that somehow burrow their way right into the guilty part of the brain. Flailing for some kind of defense, I wisely sought out another teacher, a kinder and gentler one, to help me with my general lack of skills when dealing with the drama of teenage crises. The funny thing was, when I told the high school counselor what I said, she gave me the how-could-you? look as well!

This type of emotional drama would turn out to be a major factor in my educational career. Learning how to deal with it, and how to stop it from destroying the learning environment, would become a time- and labor-intensive endeavor.

The drama factor was the most challenging for me because I wanted to approach the issue dispassionately, coming at the problem in a very matter-of-fact way. But "dispassionately" isn't even a normal part of any teacher's vocabulary. Learning to outwardly demonstrate care and concern for others was not easy for me.

I'm not saying that I'm some kind of mindless, heartless ogre, living in the woods or under the bridge. I cared very much for my students, community, and profession. But I felt that making a show of it was a waste of energy and too easily pulled us off task. As I ran into more of these types of situations, I developed a series of "canned" responses to the frequent emotional outbursts I would encounter.

For example, when a student or parent would tell me they were angry, I would mention that was their choice, and it had little (or nothing) to do with me. Sometimes this calmed them down, but often it didn't help at all. Or, if a student told me (and a lot did) that they had "anger issues," I would normally respond, "Well, that's too bad, I hope you figure that out."

While the students would often get indignant with me, I failed to see how their lack of emotional composure was my responsibility. Still, my refusal to see things their way often resulted in a visit from my understanding—but sometimes frustrated—principal.

So, When Will You be a Real Teacher?

This was a question I was asked by many certified teachers during my time as a JROTC instructor. Hearing the question "When will you be a real teacher?" sounded insulting at first, and I didn't understand the meaning until later, when I saw just what was required to become fully certified as a teacher in my state.

A year after I began teaching JROTC, our district was facing more budget cuts. I soon realized that I had better get a few more skills and certifications under my belt in order to be as valuable as possible to avoid becoming one of the impending reductions.

It was during this time that I began exploring the idea of teaching history to at-risk students. I also started shopping around for a college, hoping to find one that would accept most of my previous educational experiences—at the time, I had three associate's degrees and a bachelor's degree from my time in the Air Force. Honestly, there weren't a lot of courses most colleges were willing to take. It was almost as if I had been lied to about how important an education really is. Besides, this would be a master's degree, and almost no credits transferred.

Troops to Teachers

This particular new mission involved my getting a teacher's license, which would allow me to teach social studies to Ohio high school students. It seemed fairly straightforward at first, but once I got into the thick of it, the complications piled up very quickly.

First, there was something called "Highly Qualified Teacher" status, earned through a series of exams and tests above and beyond the normal teacher's license exam. I didn't know this at the time, but few school districts will hire a teacher without the "Highly Qualified Teacher" status, because the school actually takes a financial hit in state funding if they bring you on board. Thankfully, Principal Bob had already assured me that he had complete faith in my abilities, so that wasn't going to be an issue.

The next step was to find a school that would take me while working through a program called Troops to Teachers. Alternative paths were available, but the information about them was hard to find. It was almost as if they hid that part of the law to ensure a potential teacher was really motivated. I had to dig to even find out about it.

I figured the first thing to do would be to call the Ohio Department of Education. Well, for me, that was like calling the Pentagon. No luck there. After more searching, I found an obscure state regulation that stated I could be hired on as a teacher on a temporary basis, provided I had a bachelor's degree and was actively in a program to acquire my teaching certificate.

My principal was all for it, but nobody else wanted to take a chance.

After two days filled with making phone calls, leaving messages, and being transferred to so and so, I decided to go another route. I call the national Troops to Teachers program in Pensacola, Florida, and finally saw a light at the end of the proverbial tunnel.

They welcomed me into their program, gave me a local contact in Ohio, and sent me a very nice letter that basically said "Mr. Eric Combs is a participant in Troops to Teachers, and, as such, you are authorized to hire him as a teacher while he obtains his certificate."

The strange thing was, almost nobody knew of the program! The deeper I got into the state and public education offices, the less they seemed to know. I remember one three-way phone call at my district office between the state, the federal program and our district, trying to decide if I could teach. Another major concern seemed to be how I should be coded in the state teacher's information database!

The funny thing was, except for my principal, nobody asked what kind of a teacher I was, or what my philosophy of education included. They only wanted to make sure I fit into that all-important category of "Highly Qualified Teacher." Since I had a bachelor's degree and over 30 semester hours of history courses, I fit the bill. After weeks of endless phone calls, bureaucracy, and haranguing, I was finally on my way.

Now, I just had to find a university that would take the Troops to Teachers program seriously.

Teacher Prep

I found myself at the University of Dayton. There, I was fortunate to find a great instructional staff who guided me through the process. I fell right into the schooling and rather liked the challenges.

The only frustrating thing was the number of additional courses I had to take to satisfy the requirements of the college.

I had already had a bachelor's degree in anthropology from the University of Wyoming. I had, as I previously mentioned, dreamed of being an officer and working at the Central Identification Lab in Hawaii to help repatriate unidentified soldiers from the Korean and Vietnam wars, but the Gulf War had put the brakes on that plan.

I had brought all my transcripts from seven different universities into the registrar's office and had to explain what these were all about. I had three associate's degrees, not because I was stupid—but because I never spend more than two years in any one location to finish my bachelor's until Wyoming. Every time someone asked for original transcripts from me from all nine universities, the photocopying was financially painful!

The registrar at the University of Dayton did a great job of lining up the work I had completed in the past to what might fit with the master's program. I would need to complete the program to get my teaching license, and apparently, I still needed to fill some gaps. I needed to take Economics, Statistics, and one class that I was really annoyed about taking: American History. I had already taken it in Wyoming, but at the time, the rules stipulated I must take Ohio's version of it.

I kept thinking, "Okay, maybe Washington didn't cross the Delaware." The strangest thing about that course was when I showed up the first day, one of my seniors in JROTC was also in the class. When she saw me, she excitedly assumed I was teaching the course! I had to awkwardly let the professor know why I was there, and that I wasn't there to usurp his class. I also did discover that my course in Wyoming was correct—Washington's maneuvers did, in fact, occur in 1776.

I took all my courses, in addition to several other exams not required by regular teachers, to make sure I was "appropriate" for K-12 education. One was called the Haberman Test, and it was quite an odd test. The results showed that while I was a good candidate to be a teacher, I might have difficulty with the bureaucracy of working in a government setting. You have to keep an eye on those free thinkers!

Another odd detail about becoming a teacher was the requirement of unpaid student teaching. The expectation is that all those seeking the coveted license should be in the classroom as much as possible before becoming a teacher. It made sense to me. However, in my circumstance, I wasn't a young person still in college. I had a teenager in high school and a family to support! Thankfully, because I was teaching history in my JROTC classes and I had regular visits from my supervisors, my classroom teaching qualified as student teaching.

After all the classes were done, the last hurdle I had before me was the completion of the Praxis Exam for my license. I nailed the test the first time out. I was fortunate that I took the Integrated Social Studies License program when I did. The state soon after made it a mandatory program, and I was, therefore, ahead of the curve on that part. When I took the Praxis III exam, I was one of the first to be observed by a state examiner. While I was hoping for a calm and efficient day, three major events happened during my "inspection." We had a fire drill, I had one student melt down in my class because of a failed test in another class, and I learned that the district was going to be making some serious cuts in funding and staffing. I pressed on with the class—and, at the end, the examiner shook my hands, said, "Good job," and that was that.

Into the Classroom

Probably the biggest change for me in becoming a teacher was overcoming (or at least settling with) my own past. When I walked into the classroom, I was no longer SMSgt Combs. I held neither rank nor privilege. The whole "earn respect" deal dialed back to zero.

Overcoming your past is different from ignoring it, or even trying to bury it. For quite a while, I didn't want anyone to call me "Sarge," or "Sergeant." This was a new life to me, and I thought I could reinvent the whole thing. But a part of me knew that all the experiences and training I had received back in the military would come in handy in the classroom and in dealing with my new career. Finding a balance was often very difficult.

Another part of the job I found challenging was the lack of civility from many students—and their parents. I had this silly assumption that because I was there for the student, this would be mostly appreciated or at least understood. I wasn't looking for a pat on the back or even a "thank you," but I certainly wasn't prepared for some of the behaviors I witnessed from both the students and parents.

Delta Program for At-Risk Kids

My principal, and several astute teachers, were studying how poorly many students did if they failed the ninth grade. The depressing fact was students who failed ninth grade were significantly more likely to drop out of school altogether.

We wanted to put together a team of teachers, a "Delta" team, dedicated to teaching these students in a core set of classes. We also wanted to give the instructors dedicated times to work with families, and data to help these students be as successful as possible. This team of teachers was specifically trained in differentiated instruction strategies and addressing students in poverty or who were at risk behaviorally (Payne, 1996).

I thought it was a great opportunity and didn't notice that when I volunteered to be on the team, several of my compatriot teachers shook my hand and said, "Thanks for taking that on, Eric."

Then it clicked: this was a suicide mission. No one thought we could figure out a way to teach these kids. Back in Korea, we used to joke as we welcomed the new troops, telling them, "Welcome to the team. If you die first, we're splitting up your gear." This time, it didn't seem like a joke.

Right away, I started reading up on issues dealing with at-risk students, especially those coming from impoverished environments. I attended as many trainings as I could in almost any subject, trying to immerse myself in the body of work (which seemed to have no end) concerning these kinds of at-risk students.

First Day on the Job

For my very first class teaching social studies, first period of the day, I had prepped everything I needed. I had world maps everywhere and a really cool student guidebook ready to go. I was ready to "wow" my kids with some technology they had never seen in the classroom before.

As a starter, I wanted to see where they were at in terms of European geography, so I used a large blank map of Europe and was calling on students to come up and share what they knew about European countries. I called my first young lady up, encouraging her by saying, "Come on up and tell me what you know about France. We'll be studying the French Revolution soon, and I think you'll find it very interesting."

She promptly responded, "F*ck you," and crossed her arms in satisfaction with her big girl vocabulary.

I was stunned. In fact, in that moment, I almost turned into SMSgt Combs, tactical leader, who would have handled any such insubordinate soldier on the spot. But thankfully, I remembered where I was and calmly walked her down to the office, where we promptly called the child's mother. When her mother answered, it all came into focus: Mom answered and immediately asked, "What did the little b*tch do now?"

Then I understood the situation. I took the phone and told

Mom, "Thank you, ma'am. You've already answered my questions."

It hit me hard that day. The only thing this young woman knew was how to lash out at authority. Here I was, ready to teach the world, and I couldn't even get past my first at-risk class. In my previous world, things like respect and honor are natural expectations. It never occurred to me that there would be parents who treated their kids like this, parents who couldn't care less about their child's success at school.

I thought I had joined the "noble" profession of preparing our kids for the future. This student truly did not know how to respond in the classroom, and had no interest in what I had to offer. Her world was apparently filled with filth-ridden expletives and a desire to minimize her life by simply surviving her day-to-day living at home, if indeed you could call it a "home."

The willingness to forgo the simplest of courtesies really tested my decision of becoming a teacher. I kept thinking, "Who am I to try and brighten anyone's future if they are just going to have it smashed to bits when they get home?"

I remembered my courses from the University of Dayton and Antioch University McGregor, all talking about the lost and forgotten children of our society. Now really, isn't that supposed to be in LA or Detroit? But in suburban Ohio it is also a reality. It almost seemed that each classroom had a segment of kids who didn't care and lacked the most basic of behavioral assets to complete a day without getting into trouble. Lack of motivation, the ability to refrain from outbursts and tirades, and little or no support from home made many of these kids seem unreachable. And I could honestly say it was double the issue for the parents.

Parents seemed to be one of two kinds: ones who didn't have a clue how to help their child, and ones who simply didn't care.

Thankfully, I had great team to work with, and their dedication showed me that we could indeed reach many of these forgotten souls.

My first epiphany was that all kids can learn, but not all will choose to do so. The second, teamwork still works! Ahh, that truth of "two heads are better than one" is a godsend for anyone trying to tackle at-risk education. Finally, we all needed continuous training and time for reflection.

Training

Our principal was truly dedicated to ensuring we got the best training and dedicated time to mull over each of our at-risk kids in the program. We did, in fact, break new ground, and most of the training we received had to be altered to fit our situation. "Improvise, Adapt, and Overcome" isn't just for the Marines; teachers do it all the time.

Another obstacle I found was that not everyone liked change, even in the name of quality or continuous improvement. In fact, my district was just beginning with implementation of the Baldridge Quality Management and using the Deming PDSA Cycle for process improvement when I had arrived. The Total Quality Management movement was supposed to teach all organizations to look at how they do their business and then look for opportunities to improve and streamline their processes.

For me, these were old concepts: we had gone through such training in the early '90s in the Air Force. I volunteered to help on several committees and to facilitate training sessions to help develop the school's Continuous Improvement Plan (CIP).

Another strange thing I discovered was that few folks appreciate volunteers, nor do they quiver with excitement at the idea of measuring what we do and managing processes using data.

The military actually did a great job of preparing me for many of these types of situations. We used data all the time to ensure good results and prove them. I am proficient in Microsoft applications; I can understand and apply databases; I know all about organizational behavior and management. Every large organization needs these things to be successful, and the Air Force was no different.

We had a set of courses called Professional Military Education that every enlisted troop goes through in order to continue to advance in rank and position. Each of these courses involved much more than drill and ceremony. I was trained in the management and leadership theories and methods of Deming, Covey, Senge, and the Quality Movement long before many businesses had introduced the concepts.

So, it must have seemed like I was this know-it-all whenever questions about quality, organizational behavior, or continuous improvement would pop up.

The First Year

Our first year was quite challenging. One of the major issues we had overcome was the stigma assigned to our program. From the very beginning, many parents simply didn't want their child to be sent to the Delta team because they thought their child would be labeled "special." After our first year, we decided that a visit to the middle school would help us determine who would be best to serve. With the help of teachers and counselors, we were determined to create the best learning environment for these kids.

We used a lot of data in the beginning to discern what kind of learner each student was and where they sat academically in reading, spelling, and math. This gave us a benchmark from which we could work with our students in both heterogeneous and homogeneous groups. We relied a lot on addressing emotional learning and helping the students develop and foster assets in strategies to help them become lovers of learning.

We found six keys to being successful as teachers:

1. Get to know your kids.

2. Set high standards and support the students in a positive way when they make progress.

3. Separate the emotional drama from the reality of the classroom.

4. Know your stuff!

5. Try to get support at home. When you can't get parental support or help, teach the students to adapt. They need to find other people and places to help them succeed.

6. Support your team members!

We were able to get through to quite a few of our kids in that first year. I truly believe that it was the synergy of our innovations, experiences, and teamwork that was the bedrock of our students' successes.

In my post-military days, these were the best years I had in education, probably because we had the supposedly "difficult" kids that many teachers didn't want in their classroom. And because we had the "difficult" ones, we received a lot of support from within our building. We were often left to our own expertise and training to deal with the events that would befall such an endeavor.

Painting a Picture

This freedom allowed us to take some responsible risks in terms of how we approached our lessons and how we engaged our students.

I remember one girl who sat in the back of the room, drawing the entire class period. On several occasions I had maneuvered to her desk and tried to engage her in conversation. My attempts were always met with mostly single word responses: "No," "Yeah," "Maybe," and the like. She showed no interest in the class and never turned in homework. When I called home, a frustrated mom simply told me she had tried everything to get her to do her schoolwork, but she had not yet found anything that motivated her.

I tried getting snarky, I tried being edgy. I used emails and my website to see if she was more of an online communicator. All of my efforts failed.

Finally, one day when I was teaching, I walked back to her desk as I was lecturing. I slid a picture of Vladimir Lenin in front of her. We would be covering Russian history so I thought I would give her an opportunity to express herself.

She looked at the stern figure on the page and then looked up with a sort of disdained snarl. Ignoring the look, I asked her if she could draw that picture. She replied with a snotty, teenaged "Of course." I kept teaching, but after a while I came back and went at it for a second time. "Do you think you could paint it?"

That got her attention. "What do you mean?" she asked.

"Could you paint that on my back wall?"

She looked at me incredulously. "You'd let me paint it on your wall?"

"Sure!" I said, outwardly confident but inwardly starting to doubt myself. Now, a bit of a confession—it is normally a good idea to get permission, but I often work from the premise that it is sometimes better to ask forgiveness than permission.

"How big?" she asked.

"As big as you want" I said, realizing my risk was getting bigger by the second. I finally asked her what she needed.

She told me confidently, "Black, white, and one brush."

I told her she would have it the next day. It was then that I saw the first glimmer of a breakthrough.

"Wait, we need to make an arrangement about this," she said.

Fantastic! I thought to myself. I now have an at-risk teenage girl negotiating about a project in the class! After asking what she meant, she made me promise that no one could see her work until it was completely finished.

I agreed, and for the next two weeks she would kick me out of my room right after school to work on her painting.

I would love to tell you that she started turning in her work and that she became more involved in the class, but she didn't. Nothing seemed to change, and I really started to doubt my strategy.

When it came time to unveil the painting to the rest of my class, I also invited one of our art teachers and the principal. I figured it would be harder for him to get really mad at me in front of such an audience of students—and perhaps it would soften the impact of my "soon-to-be-issued" request for forgiveness.

When she unveiled the wall, the students exploded with applause, and the art teacher was floored. It was a phenomenal picture!

But, that isn't the magic of this story. When we had all quieted down, she made a simple statement. "Mr. Combs, you need to know that this picture was actually a lie."

I inwardly cringed. "What do you mean?"

She started to teach us all. "You see, Lenin was being brought back from Germany to Russia with the understanding that he would convince Russia to stay out of the war. This picture was taken in the middle of the night on the German border. He stepped out, made this gesture and a speech, none of which was understood because it was in Russian and he was still in Germany. When he finally did arrive in Russia, it was so late that there was almost no one to greet him. This picture looked so good that they continued to use it as propaganda to help him come to full power in Russia."

She smiled at the last statement and I was stunned. Propaganda was even one of our vocabulary words! She had researched the photo and decided that it meant something she could connect with.

By the end of the year, she had a solid B in the class and was one of my best discussion contributors.

Stories of Success, Failure, and Frustration

And I've heard back from some of my students who turned out to be excellent citizens and successful young people.

During the beginning of the recent Arab revolts, now known as the Arab Spring, I got an email from a former Delta student. He invited me to follow his blog as he reported on the culture and turmoil in Egypt just prior to the revolts. I was floored! He was a pretty good student back in school, but I was amazed at how he had embraced life and was making the most of his options. The highlight was hearing about his acceptance into George Mason University to complete a master's degree in political journalism with a scholarship! We still keep in contact today, and it is truly wonderful to see this bright, shining star course through the heavens.

I had another email about two years ago from a young lady who I helped to overcome her fear of heights. One method of building a solid relationship of trust and confidence with our students involved taking them to an outdoor high-confidence course as soon as the school year started. We would take them to a regular course, but with a major difference: I taught the course and was the first one up the poles to lead the way.

From the initial safety briefing to the point in which they dismount the course, we adults led the way and showed them all the steps they needed to take to overcome each obstacle. Through that demonstration and our example, the students knew that we were not asking them to do anything we would not do!

The girl relayed to me that she often thinks back on that day as an anchor for how to overcome any problem in life, one step at a time. She tried to remember to always keep "three points of contact on the pole," as we taught her that day. Sometimes the most important lesson is the simple one that brings us back to the basics.

I remember the average reading level for our students was around 3.8 (third grade, eighth month), and they were required to take the ninth-grade graduation test by the end of the year— actually, the test was administered in March, so we really only had three-fourths of an academic year to prepare. Many students jumped several grade levels during that time. The majority of our students were reading at a seventh-grade level or higher by the time they finished their freshman year. Still, that isn't enough when the bar is set at ninth grade.

We would always celebrate their success and share these improvements with the students and their parents or guardians. Many times, the parents would be very grateful to hear any positive words about their child's performance and behavior at school.

Working the System...Oops, I Mean "Responsible Risk Taking"

Sometimes it was best simply to ask for forgiveness afterward, rather than wait for permission. The red tape created by years of state, federal, and even local government involvement easily can shut down the process of actually teaching students.

In an effort to cover all the bases, these entities would pass down edicts in blanket statements. For the majority of these events, it did not, in fact, address issues with at-risk populations or the best way to serve their needs. I have found that rules that come from the state or federal government rarely help. In fact, all they seem to do is produce more paperwork, heartache, and funding cuts to programs that are working. Whenever there was money attached to a rule, it was almost impossible to implement. That new edict was guaranteed to take more of the teacher's and administrator's time, and certainly more time away from the actual teaching within the classroom.

What was even more frustrating were the constant changes to these edicts by legislators AFTER they received complaints or recognized that it wouldn't work as planned! I can't tell you how many times, especially as a principal, that I revamped whole programs for instruction just to satisfy some tweak or change in the law, only to have to redo the changes again after school started. I am all for improvements in our educational system, but can someone please hire a professional to truly look at the feasibility of the change, forecast the cost and problems with implementation, and THEN suggest it? Or, better yet, when they discover that it will only make matters worse, drop it.

The hardest part of teaching is when you are forced to start cutting corners of your program due to budget constraints. This is especially frustrating when you are working with a program you know is making a difference! Many of the things that are really working are sacrificed for the things that others not in the profession "think" may work.

Teachers Don't Get Medals

I remember vividly the different official military events we would attend in our service dress uniforms. I was in Operations for my entire career, meaning I was in the field most of the time. I rarely put on the old "dress blues," our most formal uniform. One interesting point about those uniforms is that they were like a walking billboard or resume: you could always tell the length of service a person had in the military, where they had served, and what they've accomplished during their career, all in a single glance.

While a few members of the military flaunted their "fruit salad" on their chest, soldiers still exhibited a sense of pride and accomplishment when they donned the service coat for ceremonies or military dinners. Recognition is a key factor in terms of morale, and the military really does a great job identifying what excellence is and ensuring the troops get that recognition. If you survive a short tour of duty overseas, away from your family, you get a ribbon. Shoot really well? Get a ribbon. Show up for a conflict or war? Get a couple of ribbons and maybe even a shiny medal to go along with them.

The military, for the most part, did an excellent job of recognizing troop's efforts and ensuring they took care of their own. While some soldiers and airmen abused the system, like managing to receive awards or ribbons for hanging around but not really participating, the overall system seemed as fair and impartial as it could feasibly be. This was part of our military culture, part of the tradition, and everyone understood it. As soldiers progressed through the ranks, they grew to become part of an organization that took seriously the responsibility of recognizing excellence. They also taught supervisors and leaders how to provide effective and appropriate recognition in their units, especially for significant events and performance.

Teachers, however, have none of this.

I was always taken aback when I would hear an educator announce loudly, proudly, or perhaps bitterly, that they'd "been in education 15 years…" or they had been around for "23 or 35 years!" I used to think this was rather odd, until I looked at the scenario from an administrator's perspective. That's all they've got, the number of years they've managed to hang around! They don't get medals, or ribbons, or anything to show for excellence in teaching, or working in different districts or school systems or other states. Unlike a soldier, you can't look at a teacher and tell anything about their career. The years of service, innovations, and struggles they have encountered are all forgotten—unless it makes the news.

In fact, other than tenure, a school can do few material things for teachers to recognize them for excellent service. Now,

I know every good leader should encourage and congratulate their staff for hard and excellent service, but the reality is, many don't do this, or they don't know how to offer meaningful praise. Heck, I rarely saw even the most basic efforts being made to recognize excellence. It doesn't take a lot of effort to create letters or certificates for recognition for teachers who have gone above and beyond the call of duty.

Morale is Not a Dirty Word

From an outsider's perspective, I see a very different dynamic occurring every time I hear someone claim their time as in-class teachers in introductions and conversations. It sometimes sounds like a cry for recognition. Sometimes, they are making a bold statement, looking for respect. Sometimes, people just want validation for their "time served." This tendency to search for validation and respect should tell us something very significant about teachers as a group of professionals. It also gives us insight into what we can do to significantly help these people who serve our children.

So, other than stepping up to the "Theory X" crowd and suggesting that teachers are all recognition driven, I would suggest that most people know teaching is a thankless job, but the point is…it doesn't have to be. It may seem strange that a prior state "Teacher of the Year" would say such things, but even in that arena, there is much disparity in terms of recognition.

In 2006 I was selected by my peers as the teacher of the year for my school and district. This was mostly due to my work with Delta. From there I went to spend a year with my "ToYs" of the other states. I then become a Smithsonian Education Ambassador (26 were selected for that honor). The three years prior and that next year I was also inducted into Who's Who of American Teachers. That really started my career of public speaking and teaching teachers.

Some states offer a teacher who receives such an honor as "Teacher of the Year" a full school year off to travel throughout the state and report back to the state senate or house on the statewide condition of schools and education. Some states give significant items or money as tokens of appreciation to their top teacher. In fact, a few states even award their top educators a voucher for their next degree in any state school!

Conversely, some states give out nothing more than a simple certificate or plaque, along with a handshake. That's it. And then they send the "winning" teacher back to their classrooms to continue scrambling for funds to meet their yearlong speaking/teaching requests. I met one teacher who told me that they were told they should feel lucky they still have a job because of the financial situation of their district.

As a profession, educators are not good at giving recognition, and that is a problem. Recognition means to publicly acknowledge and give value to what the teacher has done and what they do every day in our children's lives. This recognition doesn't have to be huge, costly, or extravagant, but recognition is an excellent and public way to improve morale. And morale is a key factor in the success for all organizations.

My point is simple: the culture of teachers and educators has not endeared itself to recognition. Strangely, it seems like many teachers opt for the solitude of martyrdom, silently spending their own money to equip their classrooms or to get extra training for their classrooms. I have personally seen many master teachers shy away from any recognition whatsoever. They have a strange tendency to suffer in silence, or at least until we get into the staff room. This has grown to be a huge factor in teacher retention! Perhaps because what little recognition there is comes from within our ranks and not from the outside world.

One approach for teachers and administrators to reduce these issues and stress is to reflect each year on what caused the most problems in the classroom, and then communicate this to administration. Better yet, offer a prioritized list to administrators, with the most frustrating issues on top. Teachers may be suffering for no reason; a simple change in process or policy might be able to reduce issues for the next year.

Recognition and Retention

Recognition programs can be often difficult to formulate and even more tricky to implement. I remember one time in the military when I received a three-day pass overseas. But because the entire base was in a lock-down situation, all I could do was sit in my dorm room and wait for the "three-day pass" to expire before getting back to work. It was laughable.

Many who have served in the military also recognize that some of the recognition done is simply cursory, but necessary— on rare occasions, recognition might be given only to improve morale. But given the union perspective of fairness to all, it becomes more difficult to single out excellence in the classrooms. Recognizing excellence in one teacher can be perceived as a slight by other teachers, causing an overall drop in morale. Many unions do an admirable job of identifying their teachers-of-the-year. Perhaps the unions could also look into other ways to demonstrate an appreciation for teaching excellence and creativity. Why can't they recognize ALL the excellent teachers instead of just a few, or the one?

Could the unions create recognition pins for times of service from the state? Notice I didn't say by school district. I meant time served in the state, the largest body politic responsible for education in the US. Along with pins, we could have more letters, certificates, and plaques—these are all inexpensive ways to show some gratitude to our teachers, and I believe forgotten far too often.

Involving the educational community is also another idea to help garner recognition assistance. Local universities could help by providing criteria for excellent performance, maybe even invite the best teachers in as guest lecturers in their respective specialties. Perhaps a committee of leaders and parents could be invited to help decide your teachers of the year. What about having students recognize their favorites? At one school, we had the students vote annually for "Teacher Superlatives." This was really an inexpensive way for the staff to get direct feedback from the student population. The students voted on the most challenging teacher, funniest, coolest and most motivating teacher—these were all good examples of the titles these students placed on their mentors. How about having the senior class have their favorite teacher speak at commencement? Anything to improve educator morale is probably worth investigating.

Of course, I'm not suggesting that something as simple as a few form letters and pats on the back are going to vastly improve teacher retention. However, morale is a critical element in any organization. If we can agree to espouse the idea that education is important in America, then we can genuinely and meaningfully show our appreciation to teachers and support staff. And, in doing so, we can make a difference in our current culture, which, for the most part, does not honor the educator or the educational process. If recognizing excellence in the classroom or in support of teaching isn't a regular process in your school, you may well be missing an important piece of your school's journey to improving morale. And, at the same time, such recognition will help with improving instruction and retaining the best educators.

Retirement Celebrations

Another place where education is woefully lacking in recognition is retirements. When I retired from the Air Force, there was an NCO assigned to handle all the arrangements. Invitations were sent out to family members, ensuring they had hotel rooms, directions to the event, and other important information. The officer ensured they had an appropriate place to hold the retirement ceremony. Invitations also went out to the right officials to make sure they would be on hand to conduct the ceremony: commanders, chaplains, and other unit members.

At my retirement, they went out of their way to make me feel special—and appreciated. I had a squadron review, gun salute, and bagpipes! No kidding! I guess the military understands how important that recognition can be, and they feel that serving twenty years in the military is a big deal.

By the end of the retirement ceremony, I had plaques, little statues, and a really great shadowbox containing an American flag that had been flown over the US Capital and then shipped to my final station to be presented to me. The shadowbox also contained my patches, berets, rank insignia, and a full set of my service ribbons. It was an emotional event. My family was given flowers, and my wife was given a signed letter from the President of the United States. At the end, I received my final medal.

Having seen at least twenty other such retirements, they all seemed pretty similar to me, a carefully planned event to recognize a lifetime of service. So, when I was invited to my first retirement recognition of a outgoing teacher, I expected something similar.

Sadly, it was nothing like a military retirement. We had a small get-together, extremely unpretentious, that ended with the presentation of a small box, some snacks, and a card. This lady served thirty years, and this was it? Suddenly, as I watched this humdrum ceremony that "capped" her decades-long career, I was struck again with the stark reality that public education—and not just the public at large—doesn't feel it necessary to do much to recognize excellent teachers. Indeed, many of the teachers I have met during my career would be mortified if anyone suggested much more! I guess it's in their heads to be humble, meek and unrecognized.

Teaching is a Noble Profession

This really bugged me for quite some time. Here I had found a new mission in life, and another way to continue to serve. But it seemed that somewhere in our subculture, we've found it okay to demean, marginalize, and minimize the position of "teacher."

But really, is there a more important job in America right

now than teaching and preparing our own future? This concept cannot be argued, and yet it seems alien to us. If that is the case, how do we allow the continual abuse and lack of support of our schools, staff, and even students? Why is that okay?

Part of the problem has to be the system itself. Public education is an odd creature, paid for by a voting populous, free upon delivery and yet smothered with many constraints added to the job from so many angles and groups. Local communities rely on schools to prepare the students to propel that community into a successful future. States and the nation have a stake in the schools as well. Businesses rely on schools to create future employees, and our society needs to have a solid system to educate and prepare our future leaders.

With all these variables in place, how is it possible to cram all of these needs into one package? In crafting a solution, educators and administrative staff must take into consideration the other factors involved in teaching students: readiness, willingness to learn, and the support (or lack thereof) when they get home.

Making the profession a simplistic, political issue with only finance at the center does a horrible disservice to the entire system of public education.

Martyrdom of the Profession

I think that in our career field we have a couple of problems with adaptation and evolution. I do not mean the scary and sensationalized issue of Darwinism and Creationism argument in public schools. I mean the ability of our teachers to adapt to the constant changes in the policies and pseudo-expectations of the job.

I believe part of this inability to rapidly adapt comes from the inherent responsibility of schools to be the local bedrock of a community. They are supposed to be safe, secure, and dependable places in which we entrust our children to learn and become better citizens. This would be from the viewpoint of teachers and staff. I am not convinced that the majority of local communities continue to see schools in this fashion, or at least we need to recognize different factions are putting different labels and expectations on schools.

If we add to this the politically charged accusations of public schools, it becomes clear that many teachers simply hunker down and stay at work as best as they can. A few will rise up, so to speak, but they may do this in the context of a union or other organized group and from their antiquated "play-book." This gives the appearance that teachers are not the professionals they are, but rather operate from a perspective of a factory worker.

It is not unlike the "government shutdown" turmoil we saw in Washington DC in 2013. We experienced shutdowns and gridlocks over philosophy, but, in the end, there was no actual movement toward a greater good. This runs counter to what we elected these officials to do.

Conversely, there shouldn't be a slowdown in teaching, but rather a systemic and continual role of self-improvement that is qualified and quantified by common sense and data. Unfortunately, we witness swings of the party pendulum as one extreme gives way to another, and we spin our wheels getting nothing accomplished. Probably worse is the tendency to completely wipe clean all residue of the previous party. If there were any positive aspects of their past changes, those, too, are also deleted.

We literally take one step forward and three back each time this happens.

The great majority of teachers I have met throughout the country are extremely hard-working, intelligent, and passionate about their craft. They try valiantly to distance themselves from federal, state, and local politics in hopes of doing what they love: teaching. But in this silence, they are slowly being martyred, forced to watch their profession become a toy for politics and a dangerous game for communities. Teachers are increasingly being forced to become bean counters, surrogate parents, counselors, nutritionists, and whatever else is sent down the political pipeline, second by second, minute by minute. The time that teachers have to do what they are trained to do, that which they long to do, inevitably ebbs away.

It would be great if we could simply call a time-out and request a little sanity break, but that isn't likely to happen. In this current climate, teachers are again comparable to soldiers as they face the fog of war and uncertainty of current and future operations. It is almost impossible to guess what the curriculum will be three years from now, or what evaluations, lesson plan expectations, or even grade level standards will be required of teachers in the future. Essentially, teachers and administrators simply do the best with what they have in the moment, only to be forced to completely revamp or switch out their previous work in preparation for the next school year. And that's provided the changes didn't happen midyear!

Up a Tree... With Blanks

OPFOR stands for "Opposing Forces." They have an important job for military units as they serve as the "enemy" to help combat units test their skills, defense, and reaction to attacks. OPFOR units can be huge, even army-sized, and help with force-on-force training.

Other OPFOR units, however, are often quite small to "stand in" for foreign terrorist or special operations forces (SOF) that would threaten our units in the field or military installations. I had the pleasure of serving on several OPFOR teams, and our small groups were uniquely prepared to simulate both terrorist cells or SOF units. These were intense trainings and sometimes resulted in damaged equipment and actual injuries. But, as they say, "Sweat more in peace, bleed less in war."

One time, I was on a two-man OPFOR team in Germany. Our objective was to probe a base's defenses for weaknesses from several different angles. The forests around the base were immaculate, maintained with ruthless efficiency by the Jagermeisters (Forest Rangers). Rows of trees in very straight lines told you which part of the forest you were in, if there was enough light. On this particular night, it was absolutely black.

Since we had recently suffered through a wave of budget cuts, our team was without night vision devices, and we were going old school: map, compass, and weapons. My buddy and I were known for cutting across nasty spots of terrain, places where average soldiers simply wouldn't go, and this allowed us to move with impunity to most of our destinations.

On this night, however, we had a visitor that decided our

path was the wrong one to take. Being raised in Arizona, I had encounters with different fauna that could prove dangerous, but never something this big. John, the other soldier in my two-man team, was from Ohio and had often gone south to hunt—as such, he was much more familiar with creatures of big woods.

We had moved quietly into a very dense foliage area and were moving slowly, my hand on his back since I wouldn't see him. We had been traveling this way for quite some time when we heard it: a cross between a howl, a growl, and a squeal. It was the loudest scream I had ever heard. Imagine a Wookiee and Big Foot getting into a mixed martial arts fight.

The brush seemed to explode all around us, and the roar in the dark echoed back and forth from the trees and deep valley. It sounded close—maybe only a couple of meters away. I heard John's voice shout as a whisper, "Tree! Now!" Fear is an excellent motivator. I was able to scramble up the same pine he climbed, and I was very shocked to see how fast he was moving up the tree. He was easily already five feet above me, even as I struggled with the lower branches.

"Higher man, higher!" he shouted again at me in another tense whisper. We struggled higher and finally secured ourselves. I could only hear our labored breath when another howl came from just below us. By this time, I was ready to believe in monsters, Yetis, and aliens—whatever it took. I couldn't imagine anything else making such a sound.

"Boar, wild boar," John hissed down to me. The brush moved beneath the tree violently as the beast rooted around our safe haven.

We started to take stock in what we had available and what we should do. This was an exercise, so we only had blanks in our weapons. We both had bayonets, but the vision of us "going Rambo" on this monster instantly faded. As a side note, in a movie you would probably only see Rambo jump down toward the boar and not the ensuing battle, when I am certain he would have had help from the stage crew.

We did have water in our canteens and were at least out of reach for the time being, so we settled into the tree as best we could.

Now, we had operational orders that gave us detailed plans of what to do, how to do it, when to do it, and even how to react to the unexpected. Both of us thumbed through our little flip books, which contained the orders and communication plans. Here was the problem: we were just treed by a large animal that seemed intent on hanging around.

Who do you call? We knew how to escape aircraft, evade humans and even dog patrols for short distances, but no matter how many times we searched our books, we couldn't find the section that covered "angry, tusked swine." Of course, we could have radioed the incident in, but we would probably never lived it down or heard an end to the derision of having our butts kicked by a big pig.

After about 30 minutes, we heard one more howl, but it was further down the tree line; it sounded like the animal was moving away. This was a good thing—we had to be in another location soon—but for some reason we were slow in coming down from that safe haven. When we got back in to our headquarters, we made no mention of the pig that kept us in a tree for 30 minutes.

Thankfully, John and I had trained together, and we knew each other's responses to stress. While we didn't have a specific plan to deal with this unique scenario, we had plans to deal with other contingencies that allowed us to work together. Imagine what would have happened if we had panicked? It was preparation and training that allowed us to hold it together, albeit in a tree.

Rolling with Change

How often do teachers find themselves in unfamiliar and scary territory? While it may not be life-threatening or involve a crazy wild boar, changes can cause quite a disturbance in the classroom. Even the best planner can have their day, week, or even year ruined with changes that are thrust upon their lives without thought or concern on how those changes would affect their ability to teach. Suddenly, they find themselves "up a tree" with no idea on how to proceed.

Take technology, for example. It probably happens rarely in these days of tight budgets, but have you ever come into your classroom to find that all of the computers have newly updated software? Microsoft Office has made major changes, and so has Windows in the past few years. Updating these platforms is a great way to increase productivity, but they can cause a lot of frustration if there isn't some form of training offered for the staff to adapt and use the benefits of these updates.

Technology is only one area that can significantly change. Laws, rules, and curriculum seem to change frequently, with amazing speed and little foresight. One personal example for me

is how we must continuously dance back and forth between political and social pendulums.

When one group is in charge in the Capital, our efforts swing
one way. When the other side gains power, most, if not all, of the
previous efforts are wiped out in favor of a "new approach."

When I first became an administrator, our state had a two-
year program in which the new principal would attend training,
complete online work, and attend seminars before they could be
fully qualified.

In my opinion it was about 50% on target and 50% busywork. Assigning busywork to a new assistant principal is quite
cruel as they pretty much don't have time to live their own lives
anyway, but offer themselves up night and day to the myriad of
tasks of school administration. I had just completed the second
year of a program and had just finished preparing my three-inch
binder full of lessons, plans, essays, and responses to the online
work when I received a notice that the program was now null
and void. I couldn't believe it: two years of training and experience wasted!

And the worst part of it was that, from that point on, all
new administrators simply got their license after finishing their
master's program. Can you imagine how this would work in an
airborne school? "Okay, folks, all you guys who did your five
jumps, you're qualified. However, due to funding, we are cancel-
ing the training course. The rest of you wanting the application,
just fill out these documents and you are good to go."

Shifting Political Winds

Probably the worst result that comes from these types of shifts in programs or processes is the lack of communication and training for the parents and community.

People have busy lives and, for the most part, try to do their level best to keep up with their children's education. However, when the entire state decides to change the grading system for schools, the community seems to respond with fantastic outrage and misunderstanding. We have recently seen this when our state decided to move to a simpler method of grading school districts by using an A to F grading scale. Most of the educators knew this would be difficult and would not be well received, as it also involved a jump in standards and grading for the schools.

While the state did mention the new program to the communities, they didn't really emphasize that it is a simplistic change and that the results would most likely mean that the majority of schools in the state would immediately drop in their scores. The bar was raised, and as such, it would take time for the majority of districts to make the necessary changes to bring the scores up to what their communities would assume they already deserved.

As one can imagine, when many schools received C's and D's, the communities were perplexed. Many of these districts were hoping to increase funding or at least save some programs with a levy. Not a good plan for success!

It seems as the political parties battle it out, we change one idea to the next without any real consideration on the affect it would have on our kids, teachers, schools, or communities. We continue to spin the wheels, spend the money, and frustrate those we are supposed to be trying to help.

According to my history course on American education, many people complained about the level and quality of education teachers possessed during the 1960s and 1970s. An effort was made to somehow both increase the rigor of teacher education and look to methods for increasing post-graduate continual learning. The idea was that teachers should truly be lovers of lifelong learning.

Pay

One product that came from this era was the concept of increasing pay for teachers as they increased in their academic standing. For example, a teacher with a bachelor's degree would get so much money, but one with a master's degree would get more. It sounds like an interesting and positive method for motivating teachers to revisit the classrooms for themselves. But the program soon ran afoul as funds began to dwindle for public education.

Suddenly, it became too expensive to hire master's level teachers, and, therefore, many stayed where they were in fear of not being employable. The same could also be said of step promotions (increases based on years of service) for teachers who stayed within the district for so many years. The idea was to increase their pay in recognition of service and loyalty to the district. This program has also been rapidly dwindling, and in fact has disappeared in several states.

The overall picture is bleak, leaving teachers with few options or incentives to improve their standing. I know many would say that they should want to be constantly improving themselves and learning new things because that's what teachers do. Really? What other career field allows for that thinking, I wonder?

Do we truly want the best and brightest teaching our students? I am not convinced of the truth of this for a lot of our average districts. Sure, many small communities take pride in their schools, support teachers, and send their students to the building ready to learn.

But this is not the norm of most districts in America. Most appear to be like John and me in that German forest—stuck up in the tree, with little or no plan, waiting for the conditions to be safe enough to continue on. Is that what we want for our kids?I am not sure about most people, but I would rather have my kids in a school where the teachers are supported, engaged in the learning process, and focused on the outcome instead of constantly looking over their shoulders for the next "big change" to come down from on high that will disrupt their lives.

Here's some cheeky advice for our legislatures: leave the schools alone until you know truly know what is best for kids. Here's an example: when the 2013 report card was released on Ohio schools, I noticed that the vaunted charter schools did no better than public schools. I do not intend this as an attack on the teachers and schools; it's a plea to look again at the system.

Of course, teachers are sacrificing every day to bring their best to our kids, and, of course, administrators and support staff are doing all they can to support the teachers. But how can this continue in an atmosphere that appears to be designed to thwart these efforts? In the age of holding everyone accountable, we seem to have become lost on what the major function of school is. If the school is to be controlled by every local community, then they would indeed look quite different from one another. The influences of federal monies, grants, and other incentives have changed the look and design of schools, and I don't believe the change is for the better.

Punishing Schools Based on Attendance

Why do we punish schools for their attendance levels and records? When you send a principal out to hunt down students to bring them to school, you've done a several things:

1. The principal becomes parent.

2. The principal becomes policeman, but without the authority, equipment, or backup.

3. The parent abdicates their responsibilities to the principal and school.

4. The principal is not in the building to help support the students and staff.

Where is the logic in punishing schools for the failure of parents to get their kids to school on time or at all? The rule was set in place as part of the evaluation system for schools, but the parameters are way off. What are they measuring and why? That the school is such a wonderful place that students should be naturally attracted to it? Since when did we become Disneyland?

I know for a fact that many students choose to come to schools because they are safe places, and the treatment they get is better than at home. How does a measurement of student attendance show school effectiveness? In fact, we all know this measurement is simply for bean counting and to track the money the state and other agencies provide for schools.

We need to look at how we approach this whole creature of public education and what it could and should do for our communities. I believe local control is a good thing, provided we have intelligent members on the board of education, working together with the community to solve problems and "build" the schools they want. In the systems I observe, we rely on property tax as the major function of local control. This results in turning the schools and community against one another because when the deficits continue, the schools have no other option than to come back to the community, hat in hand, for more money. In an area hit hard by a slumping economy, this is a recipe for disaster. How can a principal or the teachers encourage community when they are forced into this oppositional scenario for survival?

One recent answer was to cut salaries and benefits to help with the budget. Misery loves company, so all should suffer when the economy is down, right? If this is the case, what happened to the demand of having highly skilled teachers in our classrooms? Companies regularly pay premiums for the best managers and skilled staff, right?

In the end, the students come through the doors, and they need the best our teachers have to offer. And the teachers will continue to do teach with or without public support. In fact, the support level will significantly determine what will be offered to students. And this leads us back to what we value in America. If it is true that a good education will get you more opportunities for success, then why do we have this conundrum? If grabbing a quick buck or doing things the easy way are truly what some communities are about, then what is the importance of school?

Mission Impossible

One stark contrast I can easily make between life in the military and in public education is a loss of purpose and mission. Every single school district has their mission statement posted on walls and websites. Schools and districts have lengthy documents stating their improvement plans, hammered out by committees who have been tasked with searching for data to check for validity of these statements. But this is not what I mean when I say "mission."

Purpose vs. Mission

When I talk about a prime mission, I mean figuring out the reason you exist. In the Air Force, it was simple: fly and fight America's wars. Simply stated, the core values were Integrity first, Service before self, and Excellence in all we do. Of course, we airmen memorized a lot of other information and details along the way, but the military made it very clear what my mission was. And they prepared me for it, supported me in it, and made sure I was in the fight.

Having a mission focus does not mean platitudes, postcards, or slogans. It means that every decision made by leadership reflects that single goal. Every dime spent, every decision made, every moment on the job should always be predicated with a simple question: "What does this do to help us teach the kids?"

Too many schools are employee-minded, community-driven or, worse still, completely lost. Need an example?

Have you ever heard of a district that has failed levies, lost funding and personnel, only to have the staff vote to strike?

What about those districts that make major educational decisions based on what a competitive athletic team needs rather than on academics?

Or what about the all-too-familiar school district that bends over backward to pander to the whims of the wealthy donors, in order to gather donations in support of building projects or programs?

These opportunistic and short-sighted decisions are made on the basis of the benefit to the school district in the short term. I am not so naïve as to not understand that many administrative decisions are made based on two conditions: how we are funded, and who we answer to.

Funding

Funding continues to be a sore point in many states, especially Ohio. We face an overtaxed population that is weary of a system that seems to take and take and seemingly never gives back. Given the current economy, the situation is almost untenable.

In most instances involving funding, we answer to the local voting populous. The strange thing about this situation seems to be that the only real time we communicate with a significant portion of the populace is when we go to them and ask for their money. This is a very unhealthy way to navigate a relationship. It's almost as if we're the kid who goes off to college, comes home and then asks for more money, only to trot off again to classes, squandering cash as we go.

This can result in a huge disconnect between the administration, the local board of education, and the teachers and other staff. When schools act like an industrial plant, everyone loses, especially the students. Of course, there is plenty of blame to go around; everyone is involved, not just the teachers.

I once had the misfortune to serve on a "negotiations" committee. What a cluster of unimportant arguments that turned out to be! I truly thought we'd sit down, share ideas, and come up with a mutually beneficial solution that, at its heart, had the best interest of the students in mind. I suggested it would be good for those involved to meet without the lawyers first, hammer out a deal, then have the lawyers write it up in legalese. Wouldn't that save time and money?

They looked at me as if I were crazy, then turned and continued to prattle on about break times and benefits. Mind you, those are important, but in this scenario, it was like watching North Korea trying to argue with itself. Back and forth, demands flew with no dialogue or common ground. One group wouldn't budge on an issue, and then the other wouldn't move on another.

We spent the majority of the time simply defending positions and not listening at all to suggestions and comments from the other side.

This system is outdated, ineffective, and will never result in the innovation we desperately need for our kids. In fact, it seems that recently, decisions are invented for us by legislators without much (or any) conversation with teachers, parents, or students. Perpetually swinging back and forth on this political pendulum will continue to waste time, money, and effort without any true improvement for our students.

Big Donors

What about districts that makes decisions based on competitive sports? I remember my first gig as a high school assistant principal. I was at a home football game on mandatory duty and headed up to the top box in the stands to see the layout of the field. They had pizza, soft drinks, and all manner of goodies up there, and they seemed to be really enjoying themselves. What my boss failed to tell me is that administrators were not welcome up there unless specifically invited.

After being unceremoniously asked to leave, I never set foot back up there, but I do know a lot of decisions related to the school were made in that "star chamber." It was like some kind of super-secret room where the elite meet to make decisions of how the school will be run, who will be on what team, and who they will hire or fire. In fact, they would invite the lead principal in from time to time to issue edicts about students, policies, and procedures. They were truly in command of the place. I finally found out the head honcho for the entire decision-making process also happened to be the largest donor to the football program. It appeared that no major decision could be made without his blessing. All of those involved understood that this program ran the school. It had very little to do with education, or even the students, but a lot to do with small town politics and big-headed egos.

A similar situation I ran into was the all-too-familiar district that panders to the whims of the wealthy donors to certain building projects or programs.

I was once told that poor scores may get you yelled at, but if you screw up the Hall of Honor, Prom, Homecoming, or other events, those could get you fired. During a stint as a student congress advisor, I was exposed to the ugly side of community influence in schools. I'm not talking about the concerned PTO (parent-teacher organization) that helps a struggling school get tutors or upgrades. I'm talking about the pageant queens and power families in a school district that can drown your school with requests for favors for their kids or demands for special treatment.

We had to plan for Homecoming and the students voted for the Homecoming Court. It would have been simpler to have the United Nations involved. Soon after the vote, complaints flooded in from every angle after what appeared to me to be a fair and impartial ballot. In this instance the student congress was filled with a mix of the popular kids as well as with go-getters who were not as popular, of whom I was very proud. To see these hardworking but not as popular kids challenged by a few well-to-do families was quite disheartening. But, in the end, they were forced to reissue the ballot.

Not surprisingly, the results were the same. Again, the complaints poured in, and we received yet another call for another vote. This time, a more secret ballot was done on very short notice, so only a select few students would know when and where to participate. I refused to go along with that nonsense and didn't hear the end of it for months. I was always concerned about what signal that sent to our kids. Should we be teaching our future leaders that all the ideals and virtues we were taught to honor and uphold could be set aside for popularity or political reasons?

A Single Vision

One thing to consider: is everyone in your school building there for the same reason? Do they all understand the underlying philosophy of the discipline plan, or how you will administer grades? Probably not. Most schools have factions, each with their own informal leaders who have their own beliefs about student learning and motivation. These factions will try to lead your staff and students in many different directions at the same time.

For example, in terms of discipline philosophy, you could have a situation where a school has two groups that I like to call the "cold pricklies" and the "warm fuzzies," operating on very different frequencies. One side, the "cold pricklies," jump to any chance to increase discipline. They want to hammer each and every student that steps out of line for any reason. The other group, the "warm fuzzies," would prefer to give absolutely every student the benefit of the doubt for any reason, and even then try to jockey for more leniency. For these folks, no outburst or infraction should lead to discipline of any kind.

If the leader of the school has not set out a proper vision and philosophy for the rules of discipline, it can lead to a painful challenge for anyone administering discipline. Not only do the students not get a consistent approach from the staff, the differences in discipline levels can strain the relationships between factions, lessening their effectiveness overall.

I know these are all realities that school districts deal with on a daily basis. But if we want to truly improve what we do, we have to start from our base. We have to establish and understand our core reason for existing.

Another example of something pulling schools and school districts off target are state and federal mandates. As an administrator, I filled out packets of paperwork for each of my teachers. These were to be distributed to the teachers, who would then have to go line by line to ensure that certain recalled equipment or flammable items are no longer in their rooms. This particular requirement stemmed from a federal mandate. And while it was important on some level, it took precious time away from my teacher's planning and preparation to teach.

In fact, every single new law that comes down from "on high" appears to be designed simply to continuously steal more and more of our time to teach. Teachers have been forced to become safety, security, and fire inspectors. They have been forced to become nutritionists, counselors, and mentors. They must take on so many titles, it's really a wonder they get any teaching done at all.

Assuming our kids come to us ready and raring to learn is a big mistake. Teachers have truly mastered the "sit down, shut up, and take the test" concept already, but our students come to us from so many varied backgrounds and circumstances, we can't assume anything. What is your competition for your student's attention?

I have never seen a lesson that is more entertaining than popular video games like Skyrim, World of Warcraft, or Diablo II. That is where many students and other young people naturally go when they are not forced to be in school. Social media, gaming, hanging out in online communities with friends. These are just a few of a myriad of other digital or electronic diversions where many of our student live—and, I should add, with little or no supervision or protection.

I remember a girl came into my ninth grade class and told me that her brother was returning from duty in Iraq. I smiled and asked her what service he was in.

She shrugged and said, "I don't know. He has a uniform."

Well, I thought, that narrows it down. "What did he do in the military?"

"He has a gun," she said. "Oh, yeah, and he got a medal. It was purple, I think."

I looked at her, stunned. After a moment, I decided to take a little chance. I asked her to ask him for a copy of the citation so that we could read it in class. She agreed and headed off down the hall.

The next day she came in with a huge surprise. Her brother had given her the citation, along with the medal itself and the flag flown at the ceremony. She didn't know, but he had also earned the Bronze Star with Valor. As she read about this young Marine who was wounded while crossing a heavily armed bridge and carrying an Iraqi mother to safety, the class went very quiet. She looked up in astonishment.

"My brother is a hero."

I'd like to say that answer, or that deeply personal realization, would be found on some valuable state assessment somewhere, but I sincerely doubt it. Can respect be quantified? Or awe? All I do know for certain is that she learned something important that day. We all did.

Teachers and Soldiers

You have a supreme mission, highly critical to national security. You have limited resources, manpower, and time. However, this mission must not fail. Give no regard to unfunded demands, time constraints, equipment failures, staffing issues, or the ever-shifting political winds. If your mission fails, the fiber and structure of our very society is at risk of collapsing.

If this sounds like a military briefing, you would be right. But, if you really think about it, it's your job—as a teacher.

Teachers are much more like soldiers than most people would like to admit; doing the impossible, with little or nothing, is an average job for a soldier. I remember in the '90s being deployed to Kuwait, armed with 1960s-era M-16 rifles. They had also delivered the newest ammunition designed for the M-16A2, the newest model of the M-16. They were kind enough to send a note along with the ammunition as well, that read: "Do NOT use with earlier versions of the M-16 as this will cause barrel damage and possible injury."

I thought to myself, "Well, whoop-de-do, Skippy! Now

what?"

That ended up being be our quick and aggravated response, immediately followed up with plans on how to minimize this debacle. Honestly, the best I could come up with was running away if we encountered the enemy in such a state.

Other suggestions guys came up with ranged from throwing rocks at our attackers to using harsh language on them or invoking the ever-popular power of positive thinking.

In the end, we allocated rifles and mixed the different types of ammo in the magazines so they probably wouldn't burn up the barrels immediately.

Give yourself a fighting chance—adapt, overcome, and get on with it.

When Operations Go Wrong

The Puma HC-1 flared and settled into a 75-foot hover.

The Puma, an all-weather utility helicopter capable of seating 20, is used mostly by the French and British Air Forces. It was a night training exercise and I was the only American on a team of British Special Forces.

My job was to assist with the DEMs (demolitions used for the assault) and assist my team in recovering proof of the enemy's operational capabilities. We were flying NOE (Nap of Earth), which means we were zooming through the night sky just above the tree line, hugging the hills and features of the terrain around us.

Our team leader signaled to get ready as our helicopter

flared its nose and rapidly slowed down. By the time I was on my feet, the RM (Rappel Master) had already deployed the fast rope arm, which swings out from the helicopter to assist in rappelling maneuvers. The rope was already out, and the rest of the team was silently sliding down into the cold Welsh evening.

Before I tell you the results of that training mission, you should know we spent the previous two days training and practicing this particularly type of aerial assault. We knew the helicopter crew, our spots and jobs to the nth degree from days of repetition.

I was the last man out, carrying some DEMs with me, and was ready to deploy with the team on the right for security. Over the past two days we had gone out of that bird a dozen times and moved to our positions, executing that segment of our mission with perfection each and every time. It was important to us all that each man got it right.

I moved to the doorway. As soon as I saw my teammate's hands touch the rope, I crouched slightly and readied myself to hit the fast rope. Everything happened as planned. The cool evening air whipped around, blown by the strong prop wash beneath the helicopter.

We quickly descended as a group to the earth. It should be noted that when the team hit the ground, we were supposed to move to a secure position and take cover until the helicopter vacated the area. When we hit the ground this time, however, the fast rope had been deployed on the side of an earthen berm. The troops were not landing on a flat surface but on a steep incline. I remember hitting the ground right foot first, but my left leg stretched downward and found nothing but air. The world spun quickly around and I landed face up on top of a pile of fallen British troops.

All was silent as the helicopter vacated the area—several of the team later swore they saw a smile on the pilot's face as he raced away. The silence returned as the blades thrummed out of the night, and then the patrol sergeant below made his refocusing statement: "Right, mates, up we go. This does not look professional."

We pulled ourselves out of the pile and returned to the mission as planned. We all knew what had happened: "Murphy" was at play. We all knew it was common for things to go wrong when you put a plan into action. The reality was that we often planned for things to go wrong, even when they go ridiculously wrong.

The right reaction of the team, in tandem with the changing landscape of the event or activity, is essential if you want to be able to overcome unseen circumstances that inevitably occur.

Because of that training, I never really felt that we couldn't get the job done while I was in the military. The training was often intense, sometimes dangerous, and always immensely detailed.

I remember getting a new computer system on my desk as a training sergeant in England. I wasn't allowed to touch it at all until I had been properly trained. We were sent to a two-week school for DOS (Disk Operating System) before we were finally allowed to load the software and use the computer. The same thing happened when packages of Windows, Harvard Graphics, and Microsoft Office came; we were trained on all new upgrades. Ahead of the training, using the equipment was expressly forbidden.

Whenever we went to a different location or worked with different units, we always had briefings and meetings to get acclimated to the new area and operations. This part of military life, coupled with the comradeship I felt for my teammates, is what I miss the most.

In education, it is almost as if you are on your own. I did have a very good mentor in my early years who helped me learn how to deal with the paperwork. But after the door closed, it was just me and the students. No back-up, no team, just me and the lesson plan, the ticking clock, and the stares of the students, waiting not-so-patiently for me to make them smarter.

This isolation can make it very difficult for teachers to even conceive of working in teams. And when you add in the specter of evaluations based on student performance, the tendencies to try and work in teams are further impeded.

Qualities We Need

Tenacity

Talk about working in a hostile environment! I'm not being cute. Step into any high school hallway sometime. Many adults would be shocked at what they hear coming out of the mouths of our students. Likely, the adults would be quite frightened by the habits displayed by our nation's "future leaders." Teachers need to tenaciously stick to the mission because the stakes are high and the job truly is tough! High school can be quite intimidating, especially for a new teacher.

Doing "more with less" seemed to be the motto of the Air

Force in the mid-'90s. Process improvement and Total Quality Management initiatives were abundant everywhere, and every NCO and officer had to be trained in process improvement and quality management processes.

Since I've been a teacher, I've noticed the frighteningly close similarities of how public education is constantly defunded and the words "do more with less" are aptly applied. What is most frustrating are the constant demands to make students more technologically capable at the same time. I've got news for you: equipment, and training people how to teach others to use it, costs money.

The bizarre thing is that more money than ever is being spent on education from state budgets! At first glance, it would almost appear that somebody is not pulling their weight. However, upon closer inspection, you can easily find the money pits.

Years ago, we had a state inspection to check on our implementation of "Jarod's Law." This law was passed in Ohio in 2005 and was originally created to prevent future injuries to students from the large folding tables present in many schools and cafeterias. The tragic event upon which the law was based occurred in 2003 to a young man who was hit by such a table and died minutes later from his injuries.

In our case, when the inspectors came, they didn't even go into the cafeteria! We were cited for having powdered clay, air fresheners, and bleach for cleaning. We had to ensure that in each classroom only nonflammable materials were found. Did you know that almost all white-board markers are labeled "flammable"? Thus, they had to be secured in an approved fireproof locker. Suddenly, we have a factory mentality in the building, and having managed a small group in a factory, this frightens me. We scurry about, trying to placate the visiting dignitaries from various state or federal departments, yet I have never seen a state or federal inspector visit our school for the purpose of—get ready—helping us provide a solid education.

Only a year later, the law was overturned because of the extensive and unintended changes they were creating for schools. I can only imagine how the people who thought this was a good idea cringed when they found out how overtaxing, burdensome, and outrageous it had become. Instead of a vehicle for safety, it became a tool to fine schools, waste time and money, and demoralize the staff.

Focus on the Mission

The concept of being "highly trained" is another comparison that can be made between teachers and soldiers. In Ohio, for example, you might as well have a master's degree to get your teaching certificate today. And yet, if I compared how much I make with that degree and someone with a master's working at Wright-Patterson AFB, there is a large disparity between the positions in both pay and benefits.

I find it strange that those who protect us (firefighters, police officers, military personnel) and those who work for the greater good (educators, sanitation workers, counselors) seem to be the least paid. Yet these positions also seem to have the highest level of responsibility and liability.

And it doesn't end with getting that license. We have a requirement to continue to learn in our chosen professions, and that requirement makes sense. But often the materials and programs we are directed to use, learn, or adapt into the classroom are sometimes questionable. I completely agree that when teachers are no longer interested in learning new strategies and methods to help our students, they should change career fields or retire. But we also face a constant flood of unfunded minutiae that ties up money, time, and staff every year.

Working in Hostile Environments

Another close resemblance between teachers and soldiers is the ability to work in hostile environments, especially in a bureaucracy. I recently looked across my desk at a very young lady, a first year teacher of eighth graders. She was always full of energy and believed in discipline and hard work. Her attitude was, of course, contrary to the beliefs of many of her students, and yet they admired and loved her for it. Tears were in her eyes as she asked for advice. She asked me if it was okay to offer more challenging curriculum to one of her special education students. This student was a Down Syndrome student, one who had been in class all year and functioned at about a first-grade level.

The teacher asked me if could she still offer programs to help challenge the child, even if the parents had disagreed with her suggestions. She saw a greater potential in this child and was simply asking to help encourage and strengthen him. Because of the Individual Education Plan (IEP) process, the parents had determined what that child could or should learn.

Here it was: the young woman had recognized more inside this child. She knew that she could bring out more in this young person's life. Yet she was haunted—and held back—by the enslaving words of the child's parents: "She has no need of anything else, she'll live at home until she dies." But this teacher saw so much more potential in this girl's life and in her situation.

It grieved this teacher to be told, "No, we'll limit her, cage her in her disability."

It was hard not to cry myself. Such compassion and empathy is quite rare to see these days. But I knew I had to offer some sort of lifeline, no matter how stoic. I told the young teacher that we should try to focus on the positive, to focus on the opportunities we did have to make a difference in our students' lives.

We needed to understand that if our students chose to not work as hard as possible, or, by virtue of their life situation, had it chosen for them, it didn't change our intent and desire for the kid. I told her that we must endure—for the sake of the rest of the class, and for the sake of the next student that might come along, one who may yet be allowed to enter in to a more challenging and fulfilling sphere. In that teacher's eyes I saw a soldier, full of dedication and ready to do anything to get the job done.

Is everything we do vetted against our prime mission of providing the best opportunities for our students? Every dime, every program, book, and schedule? In my relatively short time in education, I have witnessed some meetings or committees that convened and made decisions without ever mentioning a student. This is not only a complete waste of time, it's also a political play and has no business in education.

The problem is we find a lot of ways to make it look like it's "for the kids." Money, for example, is a huge motivator for most people, and, in my state at least, money is often hard to come by. So, when someone is able to flash about some financial clout, we are immediately in danger of compromising our prime mission for the sake of trying to get something extra for the school. The real issue quickly becomes whether or not this new person holds too much sway over your school building, principals, or even the entire district.

Working with Boards of Education

How about the board of education? I know this is one of those sacred cows, but having witnessed both good and "scary" board members, I would be remiss in not addressing this outsider's view of them.

At some time in our history we decided it is a good idea to have someone hold our feet to the fire, someone who represents the "universal will" of the taxpayers. This is an admirable approach and again, the military has a similar example: the Armed Forces Service Secretaries. Each arm of the military is led by a civilian. These civilians represent the people in terms of our ancient and well-placed fear of a standing army or navy. They are there to ensure that the military does not act on its own initiative or benefit, and only follows the will of the people.

So should boards behave. Can you imagine if the Secretary of the Army made deals to make sure his child got into the best units, avoided hazards, and got promoted ahead of his military peers? Does this happen in school boards? When we have board members who are not looking out for the good of all the students, it becomes painfully apparent to the teachers and staff, and yet may be a well-kept secret in the community. Just like with the service secretary, local school board members have a sacred and trusted duty to support the schools so they can serve all children in every possible capacity. Anything other than this is an abuse of power and an ill-placed trust by the people.

I have spoken about educational concepts and initiatives to thousands of people throughout the US and Canada. And for me, the only instance when I felt I couldn't connect with the audience was a conference of board members. To me, it felt like we had absolutely nothing in common—certainly not the students, or the school districts, or a love for the craft of teaching.

In your district, you may have such issues if any of the following are true:

1.   Were the school or district rules written from a position of fear or ignorance?

2.   Are decisions made by the ruling body often made or implemented without consulting staff or experts in the field?

3.   Is the only time the leader of the board enters your building when they have an issue to deal with or there is a perceived problem?

4.   Are rules or procedures changed or ignored for the benefit of a single student, group, or family, without regard to their academic success?

5.   Is there a general feeling of uncaring when it comes to the leadership of the district?

6.   Are the staff discouraged from approaching the board with ideas to improve instruction?

7.   Does the board member have children in your buildings?

It may appear that I've had nothing but bad experiences with local school boards, but this is not true at all. I've found many members to be sincere and energetic in trying to help the district and community. But, from reading, observing, and talking with different members throughout my state and the country, I see many incidents of board members who are frustrated with the system. Boards, like any other group, could benefit from teamwork training as well as solid leadership and guidance. Without it, they are in danger of following rogue players or strong leaders with an agenda. Any organization that is fragmented can accomplish little or nothing.

Preventing this takes two important factors: a strong educational leader and a willingness to include everyone in the decisions and policy making of the school. Incorporating both of these factors into the makeup of any board will help to build a team that can take on the task of educating in today's environment. It takes collaborative teamwork to help any leader stay on track, and it takes good leadership to help that team achieve its mission.

Teamwork vs. Stand-alones

One thing I have always found surprising is how many teachers are left to their own fate. The way we do things in public education can often seem as backward from other professions.

For example, if you have a medical emergency that requires precision and experience, you get the best available medical professional. If I trained a tactical team and had a tough mission come in, I'd select the very best and most experienced operators to handle it.

But in teaching, we often commit the horrible disservice of grabbing the youngest and least experienced teachers among us and throwing them into the toughest classrooms, alone! I understand that part of this situation is driven by the lack of opportunities we can offer experienced teachers as a system of rewards. You don't "make rank" as a teacher (well, some may say tenure is a little bit of rank), but one of the few meager tidbits we can offer a teacher for years of service is the more motivated and engaged classrooms: advanced placement, college preparatory, and other selected courses.

So, when the new 24-year-old teacher arrives, wide-eyed and fresh from college, the administration tends to toss them to the wolves—sorry, I mean that class full of ninth-grade repeaters. To some, it is even a sort of trial by fire, a rite of passage for new teachers as if to say, "Can you really survive this, Bucko?"

I have even seen some teachers talk with glee about the impending doom of a young "upstart" as they begin their year in the classroom, as if they've been sentenced to the seventh plane of the abyss. Dante would be so proud! After all, we all had to go through it at some point in our careers, right? We seem to feel the need to ensure the incoming teachers suffer like we did. What comes around goes around.

I can't imagine anything further from any semblance of teamwork. And yet it survives, like a cancer we can't cure. Sure, we had gauntlets we had to survive as young soldiers, rites of passage in different training courses in the military, but we always held to the standard that we were all in this together. We knew we had to work as a team if we had any chance to accomplish our mission.

Teamwork is essential for getting the most out of our organizations. It honors our leaders and veterans, and allows them to share experiences with the newer folks. Similarly, the new teachers have a lot to offer: knowledge of youth and of the younger cultures, and, generally a better understanding of technology.

So, doesn't it make sense, then, to have master teachers mentor new ones? I have seen this to be true in several schools in Ohio. We need a movement toward a more responsive and thoughtful program for showing the new guys and gals the ropes. I am not suggesting some kind of mandated program, thrust upon every district. We have enough of that already!

Educational leaders would do well to encourage seasoned teachers to pull the new ones under their wings and offer them advice and guidance. Create a mentoring program, or allow your master teachers to identify and sponsor particular areas of professional development. What about having a time for all teachers to share successes and frustrations during their professional development days to help build collegiality among the ranks? I've seen a lot of districts hire "experts" from the outside to do training, and this training is often valuable and appreciated in many ways. But I remember at my first school that we asked the teachers themselves if they would come up with training and strategies for the rest of the school. It was amazing to see these teachers shine, just because they were asked to share their experiences. Every school has fantastic teachers doing amazing things in the classroom. Allowing those teachers to display their craft may well set off new sparks of motivation and ideas throughout the staff.

I believe that internal mockery and derision are the natural inclination in those who serve the greater good. Those who sacrifice their lives to others often see the worst of society. Before you fast-rope out of a helicopter, it can be satisfying to remind your buddy that you hope he survives this one, or to point and laugh at him when his gas mask isn't properly sealed in the gas training chamber. It's human nature to rib others. I understand that nurses, medics, firefighters, and soldiers often share this trait of morbid humor—it comes from a need to cover up our sense of fear or frustration, and to help release pent-up emotions.

This coping mechanism is sometimes seen in teachers as well, and it would likely be looked down upon by members of the outside community. But this response is quite natural and should be better understood.

With the increase of issues of inappropriate texting, Facebook, and YouTube incidents, as well as Twitter, SnapChat, and Instagram, it's getting more and more difficult for teachers to have a place to vent or release stress without having the community or perhaps the entire world watching.

I used to believe that I hated anything to do with politics. But this would be a silly position to take, as every teacher must watch their actions 24/7, as if they were perpetually a presidential candidate. People seem to have this bizarre sense that teachers should somehow be above it all, completely ignorant of what goes on around them. Teachers face a much more stringent set of rules they must abide by than those of the general populous. For example, if two "regular" people get into an altercation, it is no big deal. But if one of those people is a teacher, school administrator, or support staff, it makes the front page of the local newspaper every time. Why is that?

When we hold people up in such a high standard, it is confusing to see how they are actually treated in a day-to-day setting. Cops have it the same way: they are abused verbally, day in and day out, until one does something heroic. When that happens, they get a little love tossed their way, but it doesn't last long. Our communal memory seems to conveniently remember the bad all the time and quickly forget the good most of the time.

Dealing with Gross Buffoon-ery

When I became an administrator, I had imagined that I would be helping more kids and helping teachers with their craft within their classrooms. The allure of leading and trying to have the biggest effect on a larger population is what drew me in. But, in my experience, I couldn't have been more wrong.

People have a notion that teachers and administrators are aligned with similar goals of teaching kids and keeping the school a safe and joyous place to learn, but I never really saw that in my years as a principal.

What I did see was frustration, pain, and a yearning to do better, all while struggling within an archaic system that bogs down and stymies every single attempt for improvement. What was probably the most difficult element I dealt with was the fact that after I went and earned a second master's degree for this job, literally every single thing I had previously learned was not in any way applicable. I learned a lot of good information: servant leadership (where the leader serves the organization and mission rather than dictate from on high), cooperation and collaboration, data-driven management, and building a cohesive group within a learning environment.

But it soon became apparent to me that the powers-that-be hadn't attended the same school and certainly did not adhere to the same tenets of leadership that seemed important to me or to the university and researchers where I had learned. That was a nice way of saying that I didn't get along so well with a couple of powerful people. I guess I have a nasty habit of forgetting to turn on my politically correct verbal filter.

Bureaucratic Nonsense

I understand that when a government sets up a program, there will be plenty of oversight and some overlapping of duties and responsibilities. That makes sense. But I found many examples of simply stupid ideas forced upon teachers and administrators from within and without the K-12 profession. Granted, I dealt with my share of ignorance in the military, but those experiences were often short-lived, and, once recognized as buffoonery, they were canceled, changed, or removed.

Two levels of buffoonery cause us pain: those things inflicted upon us by our own leaders, and those dictated from without. The latter is something we all must deal with: it is the normal nonsense and a result of government controls, rules, or legislative action. These incidents of buffoonery are often sporadic and must simply be dealt with.

The former type of buffoonery, however, is much more damaging to unit morale and cohesion. When a person from your own organization, even if they are at the top, starts abusing the organization, the problems become much more difficult to handle. Employees feel betrayed when the leader of an organization makes capricious and nonsensical decisions on operations and how we do our jobs.

In emergencies and high stress situations, we always fail to the level of our training. If it is good training, then we tend to react accordingly. Police officers, firefighters, and soldiers all go through intense levels of training with their equipment and their teammates. How much training, aside from the degree, do we offer our teachers? Are they afforded the time to become masters of their technology, new methods of instruction, and, most importantly, to work with one another?

Teachers are specialists and they should be afforded three things:

1. Proper training on all equipment to use in the classroom

2. Uninterrupted planning and practice time

3. Freedom from minutiae that takes away from their prime mission

Patrol Leader

Our system often robs teaching time and marginalizes the role of the educator. In the military, economy of force means "using the right troops to do the right job saves time, effort, and lives." Another quote to remember: Training means you "sweat more in peace, bleed less in war."

For example, as a young NCO (Non-Commissioned Officer) in Germany, I was responsible for my patrol and fire teams. A fire team consists of five soldiers who work as a team in the field; a patrol team is made up of three to seven fire teams.

In order to become a patrol leader, you have to have been trained and certified. The only exception is if a person who outranks you decides to take over by virtue of an order. Mind you, patrol leader school is weeks of training and operating in the field; you must perform many different and difficult tasks in order to become certified. Some of the operations to be mastered include tactical communications, calls for support (air, ground, and artillery), fire and maneuvering, and performing many different types of missions, including reconnaissance, assault, support, and raids. Clearly, learning all of these different skills becomes a source of pride and procedure when a young NCO makes it to patrol leader. Everyone around them knows and recognizes that the patrol leader has been thoroughly trained and ready to take command of that group.

One crisp fall morning, I went to our sector command post—a tent with the group's leaders—to get my morning patrol orders. We were participating in a two to four week field training exercise involving almost every possible operation you could imagine, practicing to defend our installation and conduct combat operations effectively against any possible enemy.

When I went inside, I saw my flight sergeant roll his eyes and give me my orders. Standing next to him was a brand new lieutenant. As an officer, he officially outranked everyone who was enlisted, but the problem was that my flight sergeant had over 20 years of experience, including two tours in Vietnam, and he recently returned from serving in Central America.

This lieutenant, often called LT if they are kindly regarded, had exactly zero field experience, and everyone knew it.

I could tell immediately that this wasn't going to be fun as the lieutenant started to give me my mission brief and warning order. A warning order tells you that a mission is now required and this is what you must accomplish. I was assigned a reconnaissance mission, a type of mission not normally given in daylight hours because it is particularly difficult to be stealthy during daylight. AND the lieutenant was going with me for indoctrination.

I started to protest, but the sergeant gave me the "don't bother" look. I had a lot of respect for him and understood that it was simply something I had to do. I left the tent with the butter bar in tow (second lieutenants have a gold bar as their rank insignia, thus they are referred to as butter bars).

We had been conducting the exercise for about a week, so I started explaining what we'd done so far, but he wasn't interested and started talking at me from the beginning and never let up. He reminded me that he had a degree in nutrition and that he was in fact an Air Force Academy graduate. Each time he did, he would show me the blue gemmed academy ring on his finger. I really did the best I could to be respectful, I promise!

I rallied up my troops to carry out the three team fire patrol and started giving out the warning order so they could prepare for the mission.

I gave them their coordinates and started writing out the patrol order, the plans for exactly what we are to do, when and how. All of this was done despite the constant jabbering of our young lieutenant. Forty minutes passed and my team reassembled, having prepared their gear and weapons, and the new lieutenant interrupted the final orders with one screeching command: "Sergeant, I will be taking command of this patrol. As an Academy grad, I have been trained to do so."

I looked at my guys and then at the young Academy grad. "Sir, no offense, but I've been to patrol leader school and have been with this team for almost a year. It's best you observe and learn while we conduct this recon."

He looked perplexed that I simply didn't give in. "You don't understand, sergeant," he said. "I am giving you an order. I am taking charge and I don't want to hear another word from you!"

Thank God this was just an exercise where no one could actually be killed, I thought to myself, and nodded.

We moved out under the direction of our new "leader," and I kept as silent as the grave. As soon as we moved to our defensive line, the first challenge came. The base defense team halted our team. Our new leader had led us to the wrong exit point and the base defense team was not expecting us.

The lieutenant started his ranting with the base defense guys, who immediately interrupted him to remind the butter bar they didn't work for him. They already had their orders. It took us another 45 minutes to move to the correct exit location. Twice, I started to mention some ideas to our new leader, but he quickly shushed me, again showing me his ring.

After 20 minutes outside the wire—this is when you leave your base defense area and are in "enemy" territory—it was quite clear our "leader" had little or no land navigation skills. This all happened in the time before GPS, and we still used maps and compasses to navigate and coordinate our operations in the field.

We finally made it to our first objective, one of three, and the lieutenant gave us the sign to rally around him.

Now, my guys had been trained to immediately find a position of cover and face outward in a defensive posture to protect the entire team. This concept thoroughly confused the butter bar, and he kept whisper-screaming for them to turn around and pay attention to him. It took a lot of hushed arguing to convince him that turning around and staring at him was not a good idea, and that they could hear him fine.

So, with my team in a small circle facing outward, as they had been trained, and me and the butter bar in the middle, he proceeded to announce that he would be doing a "leader's reconnaissance" of the area—alone.

One of the guys snickered to himself.

The lieutenant harshly whispered, "Who did that? Who's laughing?" I interrupted to ask him if he had ever conducted a leader's recon, and which member would be going with him since we always moved in pairs.

"Sergeant Combs, you have been countermanding my authority this entire patrol," he barked at me. "You are to sit here while I conduct this recon! Is that clear?" Without waiting for an answer, he stomped off alone into the woods in the direction of our objective. I immediately dispersed my soldiers into a much better concealed position and waited.

It didn't take long when we heard a dog barking frantically, followed by a loud voice command. "Halt, do not move!" the voice shouted. "My dog is trained to attack on command!"

Our "leader" had walked straight into a K-9 patrol.

Our standard operating procedure (SOP) during exercises was to do as the K-9 patrol commands since you've obviously been compromised as part of the training exercise. Apparently, the lieutenant didn't know this SOP. Or care.

"I am a lieutenant, United States...", the butter bar began to say.

"Do NOT move or speak," the K-9 patrol interrupted him again. "My dog is trained to—"

"I am an Academy grad!"

What we heard next was a mixture of screaming, growling, and various other sounds associated with a knucklehead trying to evade a K-9 patrol. Our "leader" had apparently turned to run away from the K-9 patrol and ran straight into razor wire, a fence made with barbed wire but with razor-like edges instead of points. He had fallen face-first into the razor wire and now was screaming.

We heard a controller yelling, "Stand down." The controller is an appointed overseer of the exercise who could stop action, warn of safety hazards, and provide overall protection of the troops during the exercise command.

My patrol quietly moved out and headed to the next objective. We completed the other two and headed back to our command post. When I went into the tent to make my report, a lot of other people were in the little tent, all with officer ranks on their shoulders. My flight sergeant was grinning from ear to ear as I got the after-action report.

Apparently the little ring on his finger hadn't saved our "leader" from the K-9 patrol, or the razor wire, or even his own hubris.

Just because you are in charge, it does not make you automatically right, perfect, or even remotely effective. It may define your paycheck, or how much misery you can rain down on those around you, but true leadership needs to be earned. Leaders don't take charge when they don't know the mission. They listen to the most experienced people around them and rely on their team to get the job done quickly and efficiently. The most important job of any leader is not the right to make overarching decisions. The leader's most important function is to inspire their troops, gain their confidence, and then make the best decisions with the mission and troops in mind.

The very same goes for administrators and superintendents. The position alone gives you little if you don't earn the right to make the best decisions. The very best leaders I witnessed in both the Air Force and in the field of education were the ones who never forgot the "teacher and student" element of education. They were servant leaders who understood the classroom and their communities, and they worked tirelessly to provide the best atmosphere in which everyone can work and innovate and succeed.

Bureaucratic Hoops

Here are a few of the bureaucratic hoops we are forced to jump through:

BCI Check

Each time we have to pay for our licenses, I have noticed a most idiotic scenario. Once you've done all your additional education and training, we have to pay for a background criminal investigation. While I completely agree that is a great idea, it is how they conduct the check that baffles me. They take your fingerprints again.

It seems really odd that they simply can't plug in my name or social security number to figure this out, but somehow they plug in a new set of fingerprints. What also confuses me is, didn't they save the last ones? Aren't those fingerprints already on file somewhere? I asked the lady at one location why they did the resubmission of prints, but she couldn't answer. Seems like a huge waste of money and time to me.

Increased and Changed Licensure Requirements

There also seems to be an ever-increasing number of changes to our licenses and how long we may keep them. When the "powers that be" change the rules, it is often confusing to try to find out if you still qualify, and what else you have to do to keep up with the Department of Education requirements.

To make matters worse, having been an alternative license holder through the Troops to Teachers program, a black hole seemed to have opened up and erased any information about particular programs.

Unfunded Requests

Unfunded requests are probably the most frustrating invasion of insanity in our schools. If a legislator comes up with some bill or law, plugs it in, and it passes through committees and eventually creates some bizarre idea that has everything to do with increasing the workload and time spent on the items with no way to fund it.

When schools are hit with these unfunded requests, staff tend to scatter to the four winds, trying to find a way to adhere to the new "law" or rule. Tensions are raised and the inevitable question of "Where do we cut again?" creates havoc and reduces the school's ability to offer their classes and support for students.

Here are two examples:

We were informed about a new rule called the "Third Grade Guarantee," in which each school was to ensure all children were reading at a level determined by a single test given by the state. If the student did not read at the required level, they were to be held back in third grade until they were able to pass the exam. Now, given that all students mature at different rates and learn in different ways, this testing program quickly became a difficult scenario.

The knockout punch? Deciding what to do with the students who are held back. What if your school (as ours was) is packed to the rafters with kids and you have no more classrooms? Where will these kids go? Who will teach them up to the exam so they can pass on to fourth grade?

In addition to this program, schools were also required to offer additional assistance, both inside and outside the school, to each child who wasn't performing at grade level. While there are a lot of nice people out there helping our schools—volunteers, churches, etc.—there aren't any "free" options for professional tutoring when mandated by the state.

Again, because of unfunded mandates and requests forced upon us from "on high," we are forced to cut deeper into our already-dwindling budgets. The specter of hiring off-site tutors that were not part of the school—another requirement of the law—really bit us hard as we tried to find appropriate, state-approved resources that we could afford.

Obesity Checks

Obesity checks for students was another stellar program that caused quite a bit of heartache in schools. A ruling that came down that schools were to weigh and report the body mass index of every student to the state and their parents. Happily, this requirement died off quickly with a resolution that made it "optional."

While I understand the importance of having a healthy populous, who made the schools the arbiter of gluttony? I was not excited about having to create a list of students who didn't meet the standards and then having to notify the parents. If we are supposed to be community builders, how does this help? And again, this was to be done without additional funds to collect, track, and report the data and information.

How people in charge make decisions without considering the consequences to others really does confuse me. Schools are systems, and systems can be quite complicated. When someone "on high" makes a change, sometimes even a slight one, the ripple effects can be catastrophic to many other areas within the system. To advise, recommend, or dictate changes without considering the effects on all involved is naive at best—and downright irresponsible for those who profess to know how to make such changes. It shows a great lack of knowledge of how the schools work and are funded by those who really should know the process.

Computer Tests for Third Graders

We also were told of a new plan to have all tests given electronically by computer. While I applauded the effort to go paperless, and feedback will probably be faster by using computers, what were we testing with third graders? Were we testing reading, math, or their ability to interact with the technology? When the word came down, we were also informed that our current computer labs—paid for by a grant–were suddenly insufficient and that entirely new machines would be needed. So what are we supposed to do? The money could easily have added up to over $75,000 to equip our computer labs and create workstations for our 1,500 kids.

Blind Edicts from "On High"

Every teacher has a finite amount of time to teach each class. Every interruption, additional task, and duty gnaws away at that time. At the elementary level, the majority of time is spent on math and reading, but in Ohio, for example, teachers are required to either teach science and social studies/civics separately or combined within the reading and math lessons. All subjects are well and good, and I definitely believe in blending them (art, music, PE, and the core subjects) into each lesson, if possible.

Then technology, character education, monthly themes, and other topics are added. If you haven't spent at least a day inside an elementary or high school, you probably shouldn't be switching up their schedules. These blind edicts truly do more harm than good, causing chaos, frustration, and interruptions. Don't get me wrong—I love innovation. It just needs to be done smartly.

Here are seven ideas legislators could use:

1.   Create innovations by consulting with active and retired educators.

2.   Time the implementation with the school year, giving plenty of time prior to work through the bugs.

3.   Be truly open to feedback (not just feedback from a single political party). Consider using a test phase to see if your idea will work in different school settings.

4.   Carefully determine any metric or other yardstick that your program relies on to measure success or progress.

5.   Have a way to mitigate or deal with the disruption and budgetary issues your changes may cause.

6.   Ensure your changes support both students AND teachers.

7.   Stop with the pendulum changes that simply parrot a particular political stance. Instead, look for real change based on data and based on the populous. Every time a political party moves in, there shouldn't be a giant shift in all that we do. This wastes time and a lot of money and will likely be rolled back or replaced after the next election.

Time Wasters and Lesson Stealers

There is a term used by Carl von Clausewitz in his classic treatise On War called the economy of force. His definition: "Every unnecessary expenditure of time, every unnecessary detour, is a waste of power, and therefore contrary to the principles of strategy" (von Clausewitz, 1968).

If we were to transpose the term power for teaching time, we could see a useful application. Why do we pile on so many other non-teaching responsibilities on the schools and on the teachers? And when they manage to carry out all of the tasks given, critics suddenly berate them for not doing the teaching!

In the military, you don't send your least trained troops to the worst battles. In fact, that's why we have Special Operations Forces (SOF), to deal with the complicated and difficult missions that need more than just brute force. I believe we need to be treating teachers more like SOF troops. Teachers, especially those who specialize in particularly difficult missions, should be afforded three things:

- Proper training on all equipment to use in the classroom

- Uninterrupted planning and practice time

- Freedom from minutiae that takes away from their primary mission

Doing anything else is simply a waste of time and money. By piling on additional responsibilities, you weaken their primary function by stealing time, training, and resources away that would be better used for the sole function of teaching.

Take a mechanic, for example. Let's say you bring your car in to get four new tires put on. But, after they start, you tell them they also need to first vacuum the car, wash it, file the paperwork for the insurance and registration information, and shine the hubcaps. The question would be, why ask a highly skilled mechanic to do those things?

Scheduled Time Wasting

Do you pay master's level teachers to be study hall monitors? This crime is committed by many, simply because it's easy to assign a teacher to it, wrongly thinking they have some "free" time while performing this duty. This position is a glorified guard, doing nothing much but monitoring a mini-stalag in the school. Here's an idea: how about hiring an aide to do this and keep the teacher for that "teaching" thing they do?

Here's another idea: get rid of time wasters like study halls and add classes instead, or offer modified schedules for seniors to go to work or college, or remedial courses to help students catch up.

Are teachers doing non-instructional duties like parking lots, cafeteria, and hallways? One caveat here, this means do they simply stand there looking their watches during this time, wasting everyone's time? Nothing is wrong with having teachers in the halls and lunch room IF they are there to build relationships and interact with their charges. Having teachers stand at the doors or halls with no purpose is a waste of time, too!

How many times do we interrupt the classroom for non-instructional issues? Save all announcements for a single moment during the day to prevent unneeded interruptions to classes.

Leaders, Leadership, or the Lack Thereof...

Being a value-driven leader is important only if your values are worthy of serving your students and staff. If they have any other purpose, then, as a leader, you would be hard-pressed to make decisions that would be ethical. There seems to be a paucity of leaders who make focused decisions based on ethical considerations.

A Glimpse of Leadership

While every organization suffers from the lack of leadership from time to time, the military takes great strides to prepare its leaders in many different ways. Professional military schools dedicate themselves to developing organizational and leadership skills of their officers and Non-Commissioned Officers (NCOs). Additionally, they send prospective leaders to leading schools of thought to help prepare them for any eventuality. Many civilians are surprised to hear we were trained in organizational development, theory and behaviors such as Senge's Fifth Discipline (dealing with systemic change), Covey's Seven Habits of Highly Effective People, and Baldridge/Deming and Joran's process improvement strategies.

What I find more surprising is how many education leaders have not been trained in any process improvement strategies, or have been minimally exposed to these and other schools of thought. Even more confusing, I have found in dealing with leaders, and later becoming a leader in public schools, was the mountains of data and research we simply chose to ignore. Often this was done for political expediency or the lack of funds and community will.

I will give you a few examples:

Professional Development

We were taught in basic "teacher training" that to engage the student, you must switch up your mode of teaching since humans can only pay attention for short periods of time. I always hear the 20-minute rule being discussed as a good standard. How many times, however, have we subjected our teachers to eight-hour training days, all lecture based, crammed into school libraries or auditoriums with only a mid-morning and afternoon break to stretch? If these studies were valid, then shouldn't we insist that our professional development sessions do the same thing for the benefit of our educators?

Research suggests cooperation and collaboration are effective means of having an organization improve its processes and involve all of the experts in the day-to-day operations. So, why are there laws and rules written by legislators that have almost no input from teachers and principals? Why not invite a few teachers into the conversation whenever we start looking at massive and sweeping changes to curriculum and improving learning?

Sticking with a Consistent Model of Improvement

In terms of continuous improvement, many models out there tell us how to approach improving the organization from within. Improvement can be made, but only if you have a stable leadership that is willing to ask the hard questions and willing to put the right people in the right spots to make things happen.

Any cyclical model has a point of return to the beginning. For example, Stephen Covey talks about sharpening the saw, going back and making sure our basic tools are doing the right job (Covey, 2000). The Deming/Schewhart PDSA Cycle is a revolving model that revisits the changes made to ensure it is truly a benefit for the organization (Scholtes, 1988). What I've witnessed is a heroic willingness to attempt the changes, but by the time we make a single revolution of the improvement cycle, the model is changed completely. This results in frustration, and wasted time, effort, and money. Worst of all, we could have been making significant strides in improvement but now they are left behind for the new "flavor-of-the-month" model.

Ancora Imparo, "Still I Learn"

This saying is attributed to a scribbled message from Michelangelo on the edge of a piece of his work. It hearkens to the thought that even a master understands he must still continue to learn. As this applies to the teaching profession, we must understand that if you are unteachable, then you cannot teach. Imparo is Italian for "to learn." We must, absolutely must, imbue this characteristic in teachers and administrators. That lifelong learner we keep preaching about has to be modeled by the adults in the building. We are the ones who need to start to set this record straight and show that our number one value is that of becoming a learner. To focus on anything else is a sin committed by those who have lost their way in education.

Those who can't rise above the ruts and minutiae designed to "put teachers' feet to the fire," "reduce government spending," or "stop the government indoctrination of students" will suffer the defeat of exhaustion and a complete loss of purpose. I hear these comments in the news, see them in blogs and articles, and I wonder if any of these acolytes or talking heads have ever stepped into a classroom for more than five minutes.

I hear them say, "We should hold teachers responsible." Well, no kidding, Einstein. Of course we should. But should that method demoralize and crush the spirits of those working hard every day to teach? Has no one in legislation heard of morale? Are the ideas of encouragement or empowerment dirty words? Could they go into a classroom of at-risk ninth graders and step up to that plate for a swing? Doubtful.

I get annoyed with those who can't teach complaining about those who try and do. And the most frustrating aspect of this recent shift in disrespecting the profession is the fact that all those people and organizations could be helping build the value of what a public education in America should be.

Educational and Academic Leadership

"All have value, even if it is to be a bad example for others." E. A. Combs

Leadership Traits Most Needed

We truly need great leaders to help our schools succeed. Great leaders who embody honesty, wherewithal, compassion, intelligence, and who always remember that this is a system of complicated parts. We can't make improvements in education with the blame game. Punishing teachers, blaming parents, blaming kids or leaders, none of these are effective.

We need to understand that when we dissect and work on only one single part of the system, such as teachers, for example, we will not be able to make meaningful changes to the system. If you can figure out how to get every kid in your community into the school and interested in learning, you could go a long way only if the rest of the system is also ready to serve. Without motivated and energized teachers and staff, this strategy would go nowhere.

And the reverse is the same! All of the new evaluation programs of teachers and administrators, new grade cards and methods of measuring, judging and punishing districts will simply frustrate the schools as they scramble to meet new demands while no efforts are made to address parenting, student engagement, and community support of schools.

I just had a conversation with a teacher about why they are leaving the teaching career field (my third this month). All three were great teachers, passionate about kids but disillusioned about all the hoops they now have to jump through. The piling on of more and more requirements pulls them away from the reason they became teachers in the first place, and eats away at their own personal lives. "I don't get to teach anymore. All I do is test kids. And when those kids don't make progress according to those tests, we lose money to help them, and now I will be punished for even trying."

She wanted to be held accountable for her job, but not with a capricious and nonsensical ruling like some standardized test. She taught first grade and realized that kids develop at different rates. I remember her as a happy and energetic teacher who worked late into the evening hours in her classroom to prepare for her students. Now, she is applying to offices and companies that pay more—for positions that involve a lot less hassle. Even though it makes sense, she was still hurt to the core because she truly wanted to teach.

A good leader would know that morale is a critical element to keeping good staff motivated. Teachers and administrators experience a huge burnout factor, especially after massive political swings that result in constant changes in process, curriculum, and evaluation systems. These events can easily cause massive retirements or teachers hanging on to the last few years for what they have in hopes to retire with some semblance of a plan they had when they started. Sure, a few ineffective teachers of that level may leave as well, but at the same time the entire pool of educators is being dragged through some plan that might save money in the short run but will not improve instruction or allow the teachers to explore new methods to reach their students.

We can test the daylights out of our kids (and we do!), but is that the proof of a good and effective education? I can guarantee we are creating great test takers in our schools in America! But I am not so sure that we are creating thinkers or problem solvers or innovators. In fact, I remember having to get very creative and innovative to make lessons that were relevant to my students and demonstrated a sense of the love of learning we so desperately need in our schools.

Elements of Effective Educational Leadership

In order to be able to lead in an academic environment, it is most desirable that these leaders understand the job, the obstacles to the job, and how to help the schools create the best possible environment for student learning and staff teaching.

The critical elements of effective educational leadership are collaboration, honoring staff voices, and being able to articulate the overall mission of the school to the community, to the school board, and to the teaching staff.

Collaboration, the stuff of synergy, must become our norm and not a buzzword. What I miss most from the Air Force is working in teams where each team member knew and understood not only their own job, but how it affected the entire mission. If you were focused on the mission, someone had your back. If you weren't, you were quickly reminded of what we were all about and then given a chance to change things. Leaders hold people accountable by sharing the vision, modeling the skills of good leadership, and supporting the people getting the job done.

Honoring staff voices is an essential element to good collaboration. Without doing so, you are simply a dictator. To honor the staff voices doesn't mean you abdicate your responsibility as a leader—it means you are confident enough in your ability to ensure that the best possible solutions are found by gathering the best trained and most experienced staff together to solve issues and plot the path to success.

Now, I know you don't have to do this. A more efficient method is to act like an autocrat, where you simply direct and dictate. It makes communication faster and you can get some things done, but doing this creates a huge problem: in education, the leader isn't always in touch with the many changes happening in the microcosm of the classrooms. The changes that affect classrooms are much more diverse than those proposed by legislation and curriculum. Social and economic changes can have an immediate impact on our kids and on how they behave or react to school. To not honor the voices of teachers, who see these effects daily, is to ignore their experience, expertise, and judgment.

Perhaps the biggest, hardest, and most important thing any leader must do is articulate the overall mission. For a principal, a board member, or a superintendent, this must be a 360-degree communication that is clear, accurate, and designed to ensure everyone involved knows the "mission" of the schools. The goals, objectives, and overall purpose of the district need to be shared and come alive through discussion in the community. This can be the only way to garner the full faith and trust of the community the district serves.

Some other critical traits for leaders include supporting the staff, having the right people doing the right things, and being visible or invisible, as the case may dictate.

Conversely, some traits that would definitely not be appreciated and could well undermine a leader's ability to build rapport with the team and motivate them through all the challenges to teaching are honoring other peoples' drama (thus not supporting all of your staff), implementing questionable hiring practices, and leading with a lack of transparency. Any of these offenses can quickly degrade your leadership effectiveness, especially in the long term.

Drama—the Killer of Common Sense and Destroyer of Decency

I am not sure if this was borne out of the idea that we are "owed" something, but I see elements of an entitlement mentality in many of the behaviors that challenge us. Somehow, because someone is upset, that gives them the right to public displays of anger and outrage that would be unacceptable in most people's minds at any other time. These "wronged" people feel justified in any behavior that may get them what they want in that particular moment.

Drama is the baggage, garbage, and old issues people carry around with them. It gives them license to supersede the rights of others because of how they feel. "I was wronged, so therefore I will speak however I like." It is also the inability of many people to walk into certain circumstances without being offended.

Sycophants, Nepotism, Cronyism and the "Good-Ole-Boy" Syndrome

With politics come games and the desire to play them with other people's lives.

As an example, some districts have a habit of only hiring from within while other districts only hire from without. Both approaches have problems simply by virtue of their method. If you only hire from within, you MUST have a great program of creating your own leaders and cultivating the habits and skills you need. If you don't, then you will suffer from stagnation of ability and will greatly limit your pool of skilled and able staff when it comes to hiring.

While it may be desirable to have someone living in town to work at the school, you run the risk of limiting innovation and the advent of fresh ideas. You could really limit your choices of the top teachers and leaders by having the simplistic and unrealistic rule of hiring only local or inside staff.

If you only hire from without, you are taking chances with whom you are hiring and could very well alienate those working hard already in your school or district. Those who work hardest for you may feel betrayed, and believe such a district offers no future for their own careers. This type of hiring would work well if you wanted to hire leaders or teachers who had no vested interest in the building to "clean house" or bring in the ax, but it is not a good way to develop a culture of trust, teamwork, and loyalty to the cause.

Hiring staff members needs to be done with common sense. Knowing the person (if possible) applying for the job is good, but what truly is important is the character and values that new member will bring to the school. How will they serve the staff and students? How will they help to bring about the needed changes and adapt to the ones that are forced upon them by outside influences? Hiring, like most processes in the educational system, is more complicated that a simple blanket policy of hiring your friends from within or from without.

What is a Leader?

Leadership is more than simply getting things done. It is about growing your organization and preparing it for all eventualities. It is about having a vision, and involving the right people in the right places. It is building capacity in your teachers and administrators so they can forecast problems and deal with them at the lowest level. In the Air Force the concept of being a leader started with the idea that you trained and prepared your subordinates to replace you or to function in your absence. If a commander or senior NCO was sent on a deployment for a period of time, their greatest achievement was to ensure there were no gaps in leadership capability when they were gone.

Sometimes I think we are afraid of the term "leader" and what it truly means for a school or district. Right now, it seems like schools think the leader is just the person to blame when things go wrong. Certainly the media would ask, "Who is in charge and who is to blame?" The problem is, if we approach leadership in this fashion, we have the terrible tendency to becoming paranoid and distrusting.

We often fail to see true leadership, opting instead for what seems strong, demanding, or even abusive. When that happens, it is nearly impossible to stand up to such a dictator since opposition puts our head on the chopping block. Having worked for such a leader, I can tell you that every staff meeting was met with chagrin, and the subordinate leaders always left with an eye roll and a dismayed spirit. You were told what to do, when and how in these meetings, and tough luck if you thought differently.

Many would think this would not surprise me, as if this is

the way it was done in the military, the classic "Shut up and do what you are told." But I never found the military to be that way, with the exception of basic training and perhaps the first few years while I was still being trained to do the basic functions of my job.

No, subordinate leaders (principals, assistant principals, deans, teachers, and specialists) bring a lot of value with their opinions and experiences. Most would do well to consider the expertise within their own leadership team. A good leader knows true delegation of duties and how to develop their staff's experience and abilities. A poor one ignores them, to their own detriment.

I've witnessed a huge separation between organizational leadership and academic leadership in my short career. I should mention that an educational leader is someone who understands the dynamics of the educational organization and is able to lead the building, or district, given the intricate details of funding, state and federal laws and mandates, organizational behavior models, and other such important details of how the living and breathing entity of a school or district behaves. An academic leader understands the learning process and how to best apply methods and techniques for both the learning of students and staff to ensure they are optimally "learning" or "learning how to teach."

Some leaders are very good organizational leaders, but they have little or no academic leadership ability. Other leaders are the other way around: they have the head for academics but not for leading an organization. Some leaders appear to be "trained" by their climate and politics. I have seen excellent leaders who understand how to be a servant leader to support their school, and I have witnessed the absolute opposite where the top person appears to be an adroit politician who uses fear, retribution, and cutthroat negotiations to get their job done. The following story will tell you a little about my leadership style.

The Rise of "Madhobbit"

I was a very new and inexperienced patrol leader, leading a very new team. We were in Germany on a massive exercise (the entire base and surrounding villages were all participating), and our job was to hunt down the enemy before they could breach our perimeter.

I took a chance in skirting a certain area that I knew was out of range of our support weapons (artillery), but my hunch was the enemy OPFOR (Opposing Forces) teams were using these edges to their advantage to stay far enough away to feel secure and still be able to run operations against us.

We moved up to a ridge-line and, as I peered over the crest, I saw a beautiful thing: the OPFOR relaxing in a makeshift camp. Seven members of an elite Special Forces Unit were laid back and confident that they were too far out to be bothered by patrols.

We were about to prove them wrong.

My call sign for the mission was "Hobbit." I rallied my guys and had them deploy in a classic L formation so that when the time came, we would hit them from two sides and then the leader element (my side) would rush through the camp to finish them off. Doing this required good communication and timing.

I took my half of the team and prepared our assault. I could see my base element was ready to go—these were the guys who would be the initial contact and stay in their covered positions to provide cover fire. A quick hand signal and suddenly I realized that I would be leading my very first assault. Although it was an exercise, my heart was racing, and I was focused on taking down that camp.

The signal was given and my guys opened fire on the unsuspecting group below. I gave the signal to "shift fire" so that our assault element could move through the enemy camp without being hit by our base of fire. Everything was going perfectly, and I lurched up from my concealed position and rushed down through the camp.

What was supposed to happen was the element on my side should have assaulted with me, moving in a line through the enemy camp to clear it. During that time, the base element would stay on the ridge and watch for any escaping troops or other dangers. What actually happened was quite different.

My first clue that things weren't going as planned? The eyes of the exercise controller (sort of a referee) were wide open in surprise—and then he immediately start laughing. The "bad guys" were caught completely unaware as this 5-foot, 4-inch madman came running down the hill through their camp alone.

I got to the middle of the camp and realized it was just me. I was the only one firing and was then surrounded by a group of very irritated Army Special Forces guys. I stopped and looked at the controller, who immediately confirmed that I had, in fact, eight "kills."

Keeping up the bravado, I gave him my name and rank and puffed out my chest at this group of rather large and hulking troops I had just finished off. Giving them that, "Yeah, you know it, I got you!" look, I sauntered out of their camp and headed back up the ridge to my team.

When I found my guys, I was livid. "Where the hell were you?" They were laughing so hard that my indignation made no impact whatsoever.

My assistant gunner looked at me. "The M-60 jammed so I was helping the gunner. And the rear guard busted his ankle getting up, so two guys were helping him," he said. "Then, we see this mad hobbit running down the ridge through their camp all by his lonesome."

We gathered our gear and our limping rear guard and made it back to base. And my new nickname, "Madhobbit," stayed with me for many years.

Principals, Superintendents, and Boards

> *Finding fault is the providence of fools and syco-phants. Finding solutions is that of true leaders.*
>
> *E. A. Combs*

The toughest job I ever had was that of assistant principal. I had all the responsibility and none of the authority to make positive or lasting changes. I was lured to the job thinking I could have the opportunity to make the greatest impact on children's lives and support teachers. I couldn't have been more wrong. Several factors made this job so untenable: an overtaxed populous who are unwilling to fund schools, an ever-changing playing field of policies and politics, and a tendency for schools to stick to the past and not trust changes recommended by research or their profession.

I'd like to think that most of the country are somewhere in the middle of the political and social spectrum. With that in mind, we shouldn't make this huge shift to the extremes whenever the parties change in our governing bodies. We also appear to bend toward social changes that have political weight. These all have influence on our public education system. If a kid gets bullied online, a sudden outcry arises of why the school doesn't police the online community of children. If a school is attacked, why aren't there more police in the schools? No one seems to be asking the other questions. Where are the parents? How did this crazy person get a gun in the first place? No, it is easier to set our collective sights on schools, since they are run by the "great big government" and are an extension of that beast.

Because I've never had a good political filter, I often found myself saying things as an administrator (like the truth), and later having my career suffer for it. For a time, I worked for a "leader" who was trained by mistrust and felt that only way to lead was to hack and hammer their way to whatever they wanted. This person saw any challenge or question as a threat. While leaders like this might sometimes seem expedient and effective, they often run the risk of lowering morale and running off excellent staff due to a drop in confidence in their leadership.

Another issue many of us has suffered through is when a board member has an ax to grind. While it is a neat idea to have a member of the voting public be in charge of the vision and policies running the schools, why do we allow people to move unchecked into these positions so they can "fix" a certain teacher, "improve" a sports program, or remove a program or policy in the name of politics or political expediency?

Here's an idea: you can't be on a local school board IF you have a child in the schools! Let's remove that temptation from the get-go! If you have a simplistic and singular, party line approach to adjust the schools in order to fix them, you may want to rethink your platform. While a two party system should give us two extreme sides of the spectrum, most of the populace is somewhere in the middle. An extreme left- or right-wing candidate is going to give voice to only one side of the community. As an example, we would punish any teacher who would teach only one side of a political platform because it would not represent the whole picture and could effectively guide the child to not make their own decisions. Someone on a council or board, in a position to guide and control the entire district, should also follow this example. Members of publicly elected boards are representatives of the public, and as such should be remanded to make decisions based on their constituency, not necessarily their own opinions and views. Despite this, I have seen more than a few work for their own agenda.

Who's Leading This Thing Anyway?

With so many hands in the till, it is impossible to truly determine who has the governing control over public education. In fact, it is probably different in every single district, county, and state.

In some districts, the schools are run in the interest of sports. These districts have great support for those programs and, as long as those programs are running smoothly, the rest seems to fall into place—or at least remains well-funded.

Other districts are being carved to pieces in the name of "fiscal responsibility," but they also have an odd tendency to demand more technology, programs, and other "costly" improvement. This often results in the degradation of some critical educational programs that don't appear to be "important" to them. As we chip away, cut the edges, and continue to dismantle programs in a nonsensical fashion to meet budget constraints, the question will still remain: does this improve schools? Many of the items being removed are the very programs and courses that are the most valuable to our kids.

I know at-risk kids, and I know that there are a great many kids who come to school because it offers them choices they wouldn't get otherwise. Music, art, and the humanities are all dedicated to teaching the soul and spirit (actually, science and math can as well), and to put them on the constant chopping block limits what a school can do to teach the whole person.

SNAFU Doesn't Mean What You Think It Means

I have always found it very odd when civilians try to use military acronyms in their work places. What is also funny is that many people use terms that they have no idea what it means. SNAFU does not mean an accident or unique event. It means, Situation Normal, All F'd Up. It means, "It sucks, like it has always sucked."

That being said, a lot of things are SNAFU. The difference between the military and schools is the attitude associated with it. SNAFU means the situation is messed up, always will be messed up, and you just need to deal with it.

Whether it was air flow (transportation) to your theater of operation, your pay, or conditions on the ground in a forward operating base (a base that is created for the simple purpose of staging equipment and allow operations to commence), we knew what to expect and were ready to adapt to the certainty of changes in our comfort zones.

In teaching, however, while outside forces impose constant changes upon the environment and profession, we also have less and less ability to quickly adapt or modify to deal with it.

I believe that because our system was designed for the Industrial Age, we have not been able to develop good responses to modern challenges. Sometimes we throw money at a problem. Other times, we completely shift gears and abandon approaches that may well have been very successful.

From where (or who) do we take our cues when dealing with such huge problems? We will always, especially in an emergency, fail or succeed at the level of our training and experience. If striking got us a good contract, we tend to go back to that tactic. If a leader meets no resistance while trampling over all the people around him, then he will gravitate toward that method that delivered prior success.

The tendency to follow our experience also breeds away the will to take chances. Without the will to take chances, we will continue to go down our current bumpy road.

Where We are Getting It Wrong …and What Can We Do?

What we offer to our students is supposed to be valuable, right? I mean, they NEED a proper education to press on with their lives. They need to learn how to read, write, process information, and problem solve to carry on the business of keeping our country free and democratic, right? These are our future leaders.

So why is it that we work so hard to offer the very best to our kids and yet run into endless issues related to attendance, unfocused students, inappropriate behavior, and political or social challenges? And why do these challenges seem to be coming at us from almost every corner of society?

Perhaps some of this lies in how we prepare teachers—or

how we fail to prepare them—for the job they really do.

What We Can Learn from a Korean Colonel

When I was stationed in Korea, we were invited to attend a promotion ceremony for a South Korean Colonel. Speaking for the others in my unit, I can tell you unequivocally that we were honored to be invited. We worked closely with our ROK (Republic of South Korea) counterparts, and it was a good way to continue to keep our ties and relationship well grounded.

The promotion, or "pinning," ceremony was a big deal, with hundreds of Korean and American soldiers in attendance, all in their dress uniforms. After the national anthems were played and several proclamations were read off by the luminaries in attendance, the Korean colonel came to the podium. We waited for him to enthrall us with some military quotes or motivational slogans.

Speaking first in Korean and then in perfect English, he thanked everyone for coming and then went on to describe how this was the second proudest moment of his life. He smiled and said, "Today is the second happiest day of my life. The only time I have ever been happier is when I saw my son become a teacher."

All the Americans looked at each other, confused. We simply did not understand. How could this military man make that comparison? Colonel was a tough rank to make, and he would probably be in charge of an entire base. This was a huge milestone in his career. Why compare something lofty like that to his son becoming a teacher? We didn't understand why it would be that important to him, or anyone else, for that matter.

Clearly, the Koreans had a lot more reverence for the field of teaching and education than we did in the US.

I got another clue about how important the teaching career was in Korea when our unit "adopted" a local orphanage. We would help with painting or other projects at the building, and each time we would also spend time with the kids.

We arrived particularly early one day, and the children were still in school. The teacher invited us into the classroom, and the entire class immediately stood up without prompting. She introduced each of us, remembering our names and ranks, and the students in unison bowed. We took up a position in the rear of the class so as to not interrupt them. The students were behaving, well, rather odd. There was no whispering, no giggling; just little kids intently taking notes and scribbling in their notebooks.

One of my guys leaned over to whisper to a buddy, and the two closest students leaned over and placed their finger to their lips, quieting him. It must have been funny to see this tactical team sitting meekly at the back waiting for class to end. We simply didn't get it. These were kids who wanted to know what the teacher was saying, something that appeared to us to be in stark contrast to student behavior in an American classroom.

South Korea, from what I could tell, honored the value of education and what educators had to offer. The educators there did not have higher pay, but their status in society was much higher, almost like that of a rock star here. Do we take education in the US for granted because it is expected and provided for free?

Methods of Preparation and Training

We have become very good at preparing new teachers for the paperwork and process side of "teaching." We are very skilled at teaching new teachers on how to create extensive and carefully crafted lesson plans. We can teach a teacher how to monitor student success through testing and how to ensure that our classrooms meet local, state, and federal standards.

What we don't teach new teachers is how to survive in this new and ever-changing world of education. Our kids are now being taught geometry in the third grade!

If you were to compare the level of education today with what was done in the '50s or '60s, we've made light years of progress in K-12 education. And yet, the problems we face today are not of their own making, and not really created by teachers themselves. These changes are most often imposed on them from the outside the classroom, by the constant shifting sands of politics and money. Teachers often have a difficult time dealing with these external pressures that have little or nothing to do with pedagogy.

We do not do a good job of preparing teachers for the constant changes. They need the ability to adapt to each new change and learn to improve what they do in the classroom, regardless of the external and political constraints forced upon us. As an example, for several years in a row I have hired and then let go the same teachers because of funding cuts. How do you adapt to such a tumultuous workplace? I was honestly surprised to see the same teachers come back after being let go so many times. The pressure and stress of having to deal with being hired and then let go each year had to be horrendous for them.

When the new teacher evaluation program came out in our state, a lot of time and effort was put into the program. Administrators and teachers alike were sent to training. Our district has always tried to be at the forefront to manage and adapt to these types of changes. I often traveled around the state and country doing seminars and coaching schools, and I often found no clear vision for many of the schools. The literal hours and days we spent to even understand what was expected was incredible, not to mention the many changes to the program itself in the midst of implementation.

It was not because the superintendents, principals, or teachers didn't know what they were doing. It was because not everyone understood the reason and purpose for many of the changes put upon us. Quite a few people took the line that this was simply another unfunded program that would die off in a couple of years. Others expressed their understanding as the program's being yet another way to put people's feet to the fire, or a way to get rid of expensive veteran teachers to save the taxpayers' money.

We had no single vision for the state of what we were supposed to do, and many communities were at a loss for how to respond to underfunded schools, low graduation rates, and high teacher turnover. We had a major disjunction between what the profession does and what the community desires or needs. The single effect I saw was that more always seems to be piled on to the schools. More responsibilities, more reports, more hoops to jump through. And all of these take away from what is supposed to be happening in the classroom.

The more tasks we give teachers that are not associated with teaching and learning, the less our students get in the classroom.

While money is often the common denominator that continues to dwindle, we must also address the leaching out of instructional time for teachers to get the job done. More and more, I hear from teachers across the US: there isn't enough time to do what is required, mandated, and demanded from the powers-that-be.

If we don't start taking a more balanced and appropriate approach to school improvement, this will continue to be our most challenging problem. Forbes recently reported that teacher attrition has grown by 50% in the past fifteen years, and the national turnover rate is up 16.8% (Kain, 2011). I wonder how other professions would deal with similar attrition rates?

Dancing Between Political Spectra

One quote I often hear from veteran teachers is "This too shall pass." They have seen these waves of changes before, and most know how to roll with it. They consider change as just another challenge that must be withstood. The "new tide" to rework the entire classroom will only last until the next "big thing" comes along.

I will give you an example. Does Total Quality Management really work? It was a huge movement in the military in the early '90's, and I remember taking many courses to learn about process improvement and continuously improving what we do. We were all trained, and the TQM elements that were most conducive to what we did were adopted and adhered to. It became part of our culture because, from the top of our organization down to the bottom, everyone knew what we were doing and what we are all about.

Therein lies a major problem of education. It is not about the big picture; it is about the money and about who's writing the new rules. And with the election of a different person or party, all the gains and advances you may have made in your district can be simply wiped away to make room for the next big thing.

The problem with such changes is that we lose any and all momentum going forward from the previous attempts. This has two distinct effects on teachers:

First, teachers have absolutely no "buy in" for a new vision because it seems doomed to change or replacement. It's just the latest "new idea" to come along, and teachers probably feel that it, too, will be thrown out when new leadership is hired or elected.

Second, teachers have the constant frustration of having to do so many things not directly dealing with or even related to actual teaching.

I know the popular notion is that grumpy teachers simply want to get by on the state's money and work to have the summers off. But as I have traveled throughout our country, I have found this is not the case. I see magic in classrooms, hardworking educators who pour their heart and soul into their craft. They want nothing more than the success of their students! The picture painted by some political extremes is woefully, and almost criminally, wrong.

Fixing Classroom Discipline

One of the biggest challenges affecting today's classrooms is the increase of disruptive behavior. While this increase has been noted, we still continue to address the disruptive students with an outdated form of discipline.

I believe that for too long we've approached the concept of discipline as one of "punishment and satisfaction." The fact that the kids are coming through the school doors each day means that we need to understand those particular kids and develop a better approach that helps them change behaviors so they can become successful, without regard for what they get at home.

Like it or not, for some kids, their teachers are truly the only adult example for how to behave. The difficulty arises when a teacher makes certain expectations and they are not accepted by either the student or the parent. The hardest part of teaching, I feel, is when you have to do your job in the face of a parent who could care less about that job. That one child still needs a shot at success, and it is often a teacher who refuses to give up that gives them that opportunity.

We need to start looking at methods of changing behaviors, instead of simply punishing kids for not knowing what is expected of them. We should never say as teachers, "They should know better," because they may well not have any idea of what is fully expected of them.

In the same vein, we also need to rethink our school-wide approach to discipline. What do you think a seventh grader is thinking on his second day of suspension? Probably not, "Gee, I should write a letter of apology to my teacher and think of a better way to express myself." What does a fifth grader think about having to go to detention and put his head down? Detention, for many, is not a real consequence. It is a break with a little nap thrown in!

No, we must better understand how to approach the concept of discipline and learn to teach students expectations and how to change their behaviors without them becoming martyrs to their own cause. If we ever find ourselves punishing a student so we can feel better, then we've lost the purpose of the discipline in the first place. How will they ever become self-motivated if they don't understand the reason to change? They need to understand that following expected behaviors will allow them to be truly successful.

We need to systemically teach expected behaviors in such a way that students understand the reason and value for behaving in that fashion. Additionally, our program of correction should be one that allows students to reflect upon their behaviors. They need a process in which to change those behaviors based on the expected behaviors that are taught in the classroom as opposed to those assumed to have been learned from home. Assuming students "know" how to behave is one of our greatest mistakes, because they come into our schools from a myriad of social situations. What may be honored in your home may not be honored, or even taught, in theirs.

Creating Value in the Classroom

Educators have a tough time with many kids because the students bring a strange mix of expectations to the classroom. Some students want to just get through it, some do in fact enjoy learning, and a subset of the population could really care less. These kids are here for the drama, here for their friends, or here because the law prevents them from being somewhere else.

And yet, in front of them stands a highly educated and probably motivated person who enjoys knowledge and has embraced the idea that what they offer will benefit all of these students in the future. It's a bit like being a medic giving a shot to a kid: it's good for them, but they certainly don't want it at the time. The challenge is to teach them how to love learning without wearing ourselves out as teachers.

Many teachers get burned out simply by trying the wrong things too many times. I knew one teacher whose classroom management style was to scream, immediately and constantly. For an entire semester, I thought we had a banshee living in the halls. Within a few minutes of the period bell, you'd hear her screaming and the kids laughing. This process was sad but often repeated. Her idea of creating value in the classroom degenerated into an untenable position for herself, coupled with mild entertainment for the students.

I tried to intervene and help this teacher out, but imagine Dad or Mom coming down the hall at midnight because you and your brothers were giggling. It was the same response when I would walk across the hall, swing open the door, and say, "Is everything okay, Mrs. _____?" She would be out of breath and simply nod yes. The kids would be quietly seated and looking around as if to say, "What? We didn't do anything."

When I later told her they were pushing her buttons on purpose, she was shocked. But think about it: when you're 14, making a 125-pound woman jump up and down, turn red in the face, and create shrill sounds because you've made a simple gesture is fun. And it's certainly more entertaining than biology.

So how do we create value in a place that's value-added, data-driven, and underfunded? A few ground rules should apply:

1.   Have a credible set of classroom rules, agreed upon by the students.

2.   Know your competition and then endeavor to be better than them.

3.   "Reflective practitioner" simply means if it worked, make it better. If it didn't, come at it from a different perspective. Being a reflective practitioner means you are willing to go back over your lessons for the purpose of evaluating how it went and what you could do to improve it. You may make simple changes like ensuring the language is more understandable, or you may need to change your teaching style if the students have little or no knowledge of the bigger concepts surrounding the subject. Either way, reflecting on your lessons will allow you to improve their learning and your teaching.

4.   Never reteach a lesson the same way you taught it before.

5.   Know your students as best you can. It will help you identify who needs what, and when and how they need it.

6.   Never let anything come between you and your mission: teaching.

Classroom Rules

A credible set of classroom rules can be critical to success for the teacher. They need to be simple, easy to remember, and understandable. If they are agreed to by the students and posted conspicuously in the classroom, teachers then have an easy approach to correcting disruptive behavior, getting straight back to the lesson. If an infraction occurs, simply direct the class quickly to the rule that has been broken and have them all repeat the rule out loud. Most students get the hint right away. A second infraction must be immediately addressed with your classroom discipline plan. They key is to not let the infraction steal your time; get right back into the lesson as if it is the most important thing in the world. You can always deal with minor issues on their time.

I'll give you an example. When I start the new school year, I always make it a point to inform my students that one of my rules is they don't get up and start packing during the last few minutes of class. And under no circumstances are they allowed to get up and leave my room when the bell rings. I tell them the bell is an indicator of time only; I decide when class is over and will let them know when they are allowed to leave. I also demonstrate exactly what I want them to do and have those students practice it perfectly. Rick Dahlgren from "Time to Teach" calls this a "Teach-To," and it is designed to ensure there are no misunderstandings with what behavior I need to see in the classroom.

This is powerful, especially when something goes a bit awry in the class and I choose to hold them in their seats after the bell has rung. The tension becomes palpable as I describe again the rule while that precious clock ticks away their only time to visit with their friends in the halls between classes. Within two weeks, my students are nearly always seated bell-to-bell and often are surprised when the period is over.

You see, I used an item they value—the free time between classes—as a point to prove the concept that it is all about my rules for their success. I let them know that I own their time. Those four minutes between bells is a precious commodity, often critical to the waiting drama queen, star-crossed lover, or best buddy, dying to find out what happened at the party last night. When students learn that I am willing to take that time away from them to instruct them on the rules, their attention is readily found.

A Note

I recently received an email from a former student and I believe it's very appropriate to this topic.

> *Hello Mr. Combs!*
> *This is Candace, one of your first year Delta students. (I was also in your summer civics class.) I'm at a turning point in my life right now, which means I have also had to do a lot of reflecting on the past. When I thought about high school, I instantly thought of you and how you encouraged me throughout my freshman year. I graduated class of 2007 (on time), and now I'm moving on to be a pharmacist. Granted, being a pharmacist doesn't solve world hunger or change the world. However, I do believe it is a far cry from what I would have been if I had not have had encouragement from the Delta teachers. Before my freshman year of high school, I honestly thought I was stupid and should just give up.*
>
> *Long story short, I wanted to thank you for all that you have done for me. Even though you might not realize it, you really had an impact on my life. Thank you, Mr. Combs.*
>
> *—Candi*

A lot of teachers get these small notes from former students, these beacons of hope and light. These letters are what teachers truly live for. The letters can re-energize us and let us know our compass is still headed in the right direction. They can also illuminate how important our impact is on our students. And it reminds us that we truly teach for life and affect our charges forever.

Do children value what you have to offer in the classroom? Do the parents? Does society as a whole? These hard questions demand an answer. If students and parents do not honor and value what you have to offer, then you have a hard task ahead of you indeed. It is very frustrating to work so hard to create a lesson for your students, one filled with multiple intelligences and technology, one that is engaging and exciting, only to have it tossed aside by a student who has no idea why this could be valuable to them, now or in the future.

Because this is a mandatory event for the kids, they can react any way they desire. They didn't choose to come to class for the most part. The chance that the students have some life plan that extols the virtues of a solid education is slim.

The Greek philosopher Epictetus was quoted as saying, "Only the educated are truly free." But what happens when the attendees don't understand the cost of that freedom or the value of that education? Many will not understand what a teacher has to offer until it becomes important later in their lives—or when the need arises. The same could be said of a policeman or a firefighter. An education is not simply some knowledge set or a high stakes test. It is a lifetime gift whereby we access our futures and improve our lives and the lives of those around us. Although many programs can help adults reach their education goals, it seems strange that we should have to fight over the definition of such a precious commodity.

Making Subjects Sparkle

How do we get the students, parents, and the community to understand the importance of what we offer? I would often be concerned that while I have a great love of ancient and world history, not many Americans seem to gravitate to the subject. Even fewer students are interested now that we place so much focus on science and math. The very subject I adore is often marginalized and, like many of the humanities, seems to be on the chopping block in many districts. It can be a Herculean task, keeping a positive attitude in the face of trying to teach a subject that is underfunded and receives little focus, yet is still mandatory. Imagine all the other teachers who put on their best, brave faces to meet their students with unique and memorable ways to learn, knowing full well that some of those students who come into their classroom could care less.

This is where the mastery of teaching is; this is where the heart of it lies. When students come into a teacher's room, it is more than another 45-minute block of instruction. Good teachers know how to energize the room and how to make even the most difficult subjects sparkle. They know how to build a positive rapport with their students and make their subjects relevant in a way that applies now and in the students' future.

Great teachers look at their subjects from multiple angles and attack the subject from every possible approach. They know how important the accumulation of knowledge is, and they know how to model this fire and love of learning. Every student has a spark in them. Great teachers know how to kindle that spark into a flame and inspire the student to set their world on fire with imagination, invention, and innovation.

In workshops for teachers, I teach a method of approaching the classroom called "bringing yourself into the classroom." In that segment, I demonstrate how teachers throughout the US are bringing in small bits of themselves into the classroom to better connect with their kids. I used to think it was neat and a nice way to end a teaching seminar until I discovered how vital these examples are to building rapport with students.

As an example, I know a science teacher who, when teaching human anatomy, would enter the room in full scuba gear to explain the functions of the aqueous and vitreous humor in the two chambers of the human eye. I know a coach who has a draft at the beginning of his class where all students pull the name of an obscure sport from a bowl. Each student then studies the sport they choose: its origins, facts, and current events. They do regular updates and post the results of the sport on a large board in the classroom. The teacher eventually ties all their reports into his math class to show them how ratios, percentages, and algebra are used within the sport statistics.

From poetry slams to marketing blitzes, I've seen magnificent teaching in my travels. Seeing how these teachers decided to ignore the politics, games, and funding cuts is truly inspiring. They simply offer up what they have in their hearts and minds to their students. A teacher creates a banquet when they plan their school year. The offerings are diverse, and they have nutritional value for the mind and soul. When you invite friends over for a barbecue, you don't give your guests a piece of toast. You set out a sumptuous meal so they may enjoy the food and company. Likewise, the great teacher prepares the lesson, ensuring that it is relevant, real, and rigorous.

Improving American Education

So, what can we really do to improve education in America?

First, let's consider improving the conditions our teachers and students face in the buildings where they learn. Let's have open communications in our communities so that they all know and understand the expectations teachers have for the students, those that the community and parents have for the schools, and set about focusing on what is important for them.

We can improve education by allowing our teachers to teach students to be innovators and thinkers instead of test takers. We should allow the students to become purveyors of information and pioneers of technology to help our industry, science, and military to advance their operations and service. We should build up our students so they can find their own unique form of expression and fortify our nation with their art, music, and imagination.

Our country was founded by some pretty unique individuals, and our government is supposed to be a reflection of those brave souls who dared to take on the world's largest army for the sake of freedom. It was thinking outside the box and a hope for freedom that General Washington relied upon throughout that horrific year of 1776. It was daring and resilience that saw our troops in Normandy help to free Europe from tyranny. It was a nation's ingenuity and wherewithal that landed a man on the moon. I think our strength as Americans is our uniqueness and our ability to think of new—and sometimes outrageous—ideas to improve our lives and the world around us.

When we finally allow teachers to teach, and not shackle them with single-interest projects and every other task in the world except for teaching, we will make strides in public education.

We can do this collectively with communities and parental involvement. But we all have to roll up our sleeves and work together to make our schools places of learning. Instead of finger-pointing, how about clasping a hand to hold up the person called to be your child's teacher? When we know how to value an education and pass that on to our students, then we will see progress.

What We've Lost

We've lost a host of things over the years in the world of education.

Mainly, I think we have lost what the function of education should be in America and in our individual states. We are still seeing schools functioning as if they were still in the Industrial Age, while the needs of our society are far beyond it. So many issues of child rearing and caring have been added to the responsibility of schools, but politics and societal whims have forced a lot of dumbing down in much of the curricula.

Or, we find ourselves answering a certain call to arms by some article that stresses how many engineers India and China are producing, as if the function of education is to directly compete with those nations.

I am not convinced educators should be used in such a fashion, but as long as large corporations have money to devote to such programs, why not do them? The question is, what is the value of an American education? And bigger still, what does it mean to our students? What happens if you aren't a science- or math-type person? What happens if you think outside of the box instead of circling inside the testing bubble? I seem to remember many occasions in our history when innovation and the pioneer spirit were earmarks of what made the United States a world power.

A Loss of Reverence

I was reading Paul Woodruff's book, First Democracy in preparation to teach a course at a local university when I realized that our country is in grave danger of forgetting what to revere. Its ideas about democracy make this an excellent book, and what struck me was the concern over reverence, or, if you like, placing the greater good over oneself (Woodruff, 2005). The loss of reverence, I believe, will be our downfall as a society and nation.

What we revere, or what we value, drives our economies and our social structures. If our society values power, we then pursue power. Prestige, then prestige. So what is it that we value today? Is it success at any cost?

Empirically, I would say greed is what many Americans now value. People seem to believe they are now owed everything, that the good life just comes without working for it. This is not the success of the past, described in our American dream, which supposedly stated, "If you work for it, you will have an opportunity to fulfill your destiny."

No, this is some kind of insidious form of that birthright: "I deserve it, I am given it, and I did not, nor need to, earn it."

Perhaps it is best to describe what we no longer revere in our society. What is sacred in America anymore? Doesn't it seem that too many people are demanding rights to defend wrong?

Time and again, I found myself facing parents and students who had this philosophy of "me first" and forget the rest. It takes wars and deaths to shake us out of our complacency to honor veterans. Similarly, only when some atrocity occurs do we start thinking maybe we should do something to protect children in schools. The instinct to do so does not appear to come naturally anymore.

Many frustrating times I would simply want to say to a parent or to the community as a whole, "What do you want?" When I did ask the question, I got answers like "Leave them alone, give them this, punish that person," etc. I would always answer, and not always to their satisfaction, "That's not what we do."

Death of Civility

If you want to witness how our society (at least parts of it) has complete disdain for manners, step into an assistant principal's shoes for a single day.

For example, as a high school principal, I responded to another fight report outside in the parking lot. Over the past week, several reports had come in about our vocational technical school kids getting into altercations after being dropped off at the school.

Now, I had no true operational control over these students; they spent their days at a geographically separate site (which brings up the specter of span of control for leadership!). When I got outside, they scattered, as predicted, but this time I was armed with a bit of technology and took out my digital camera to photograph the fleeing students, hoping I would be able to identify them later and prevent further infractions.

As I took a picture of a red sports car in which one prominent student was leaving, an angry adult male leaped out of the vehicle and approached me, screaming.

"Why are you taking a picture of my car? Who the $#%^ are you to take a picture of my car?"

His chest was forward, fists at his side, and he stopped only a yard from me. I took another picture. He got furious and demanded what I was doing.

"I'm investigating a report of students fighting in the parking lot," I answered, placidly stepping my right foot back into a more defensive posture.

He looked confused. "Why are you taking our picture?" he demanded.

"I'm taking everyone's picture," I said. "Every time I come out here, no one takes responsibility for their actions. I need to have some sort of record to help me investigate." I think it dawned on him at that moment that I had in my possession a beautiful photo of an angry parent charging at me.

"Well, my boy was just defending himself," he said. The hook was in!

"So, you are supporting your child's right to fight on school grounds?" I responded.

He looked further confused. "My boy was defending himself. The other kid started it!" His retort was heated with anger.

"What other kid?" I asked. "Can you tell me who was involved?"

Silence. Then, with resolve and a bizarre turn of eloquence, he finally answered.

"He ain't no snitch now!" The man sounded quite proud of the fact.

I snatched my cell phone from my hip and started dialing.

"Who you calling?" he demanded.

"Now, sir, you wouldn't want me to waste your hard-earned tax dollars by not doing my job, would you?" I asked. "I'm calling the police and making a report."

He seemed surprised at this and immediately started back toward his car.

"They'll be here in just a minute," I continued. "If you'd like to share your part of the story with them."

He stopped and considered the option. He decided to wait because if the other boy got his opportunity his boy wouldn't get the same "fair" share.

This example is replete with the idea that it was okay to fight, it's okay to break the rules, just as long as you get away with it. The man saw nothing wrong in fighting or breaking the rules. In fact, he was supporting it. Civility has been completely forgotten. It's not even a moot point in this person's life. But what caused this? Is this a vestigial trait from a free market society? As long as I get mine, I don't care what happens to anyone else?

Civility is no longer respected, desired, or honored in some parts of American society. It appears that, in many ways, the standards of treating each other have truly changed for the worse.

Another scenario that played out in front of me involved three girls and a trashed bathroom. One by one, I called them into my office. One by one, they let enough slip out for me to determine they had been there, they had done it, and they had fun doing it. I issued in-school suspensions and sent them on their way.

Then came the angry phone calls.

One mom called and demanded to know why her innocent child was being punished for going to the bathroom for her menstrual cycle. For the rest of the conversation, she refused to hear any explanation and demanded I recant the punishment. I politely gave her the number of my superior.

To push the incident into complete buffoonery, the student couldn't even remain civil for a single day of in-school restriction, earning an unprecedented additional six more days for misbehavior. Our policy was that you can only receive two additional days and then you face out-of-school suspension. So, with policy in hand, I proceeded to issue this girl an out-of-school suspension.

The next call came in.

"You're kicking her out of school for her period?" The woman had a screech-like quality to her voice that mimicked a banshee and made it extremely hard for me to keep my composure. She demanded to see the principal, and once that didn't satisfy her indignation, she declared she would remove her child from our evil school. Incidentally, the child returned shortly thereafter—she had been removed from two other schools.

I often wonder if we could teach data-driven management to parents so that when they see the behavior trends in their child, perhaps it would drive them to make different decisions.

Time and again, I had parents or students coming in screaming or acting as if I have wronged them in some inconceivable fashion while addressing a school issues with their student. I realize this is, in part, a manifestation of an idea of social justice that states that some people in poverty (social, emotional, or economic) will tend to view the world as their personal shopping mall. They feel they are "owed" respect, money, a job, etc., and they tend to pass this belief on to their children. I remember hearing once a parent telling his boy who was in trouble for fighting, "Remember, you don't give respect until they give it."

Students who simply refuse to do work are an interesting lot, especially given that future teacher contracts and pay scales are to be directly connected to student performance. How do we square that issue? What do we do as teachers when the student misses 20 to 40 days of school, and refuses to do schoolwork? In these situations it is often impossible to get a conference with the parents because the phone is disconnected, they have moved, or they simply refuse to meet with the teacher and principal. How are we supposed to evaluate the teacher based on that student's performance?

Imagine any other career field where your pay is dependent upon the actions of others, and those others are juveniles. I truly believe we need to have excellent teachers, ones who are dedicated to continual learning and hold their charges to high standards. But to test the kids into infinity and then tie someone's career to a single point of a child's performance doesn't sound like a bright idea to me.

What if we tied police officer's pay to the number of traffic tickets a person doesn't get? How about if we tied a dentist's pay to the number of cavities their patients got? Or, better still, what if we tied a legislator's pay to the number of successful bills they get through the House or Senate?

I wonder how many teachers face the indignant child who looks up at them and says, "I did half of my work," as if stating that should be quite enough for the likes of you. Sometimes, when that is all we get from a child, we celebrate a little bit. But in that small celebration dies another piece of the high expectations and results we actually have for our students. Since when did the idea of partial work become acceptable? When did partial work become a victory?

I had conducted a minor study in my first two years of teaching ninth graders. I had decided that all my students would know they were already average, and that I believed they would all be much greater in this class, therefore I would assign no D's. That's right: my expectation was that all students would do "C" work or better. This actually worked quite well for almost a month. All my students were turning in their work and had a 75% or better on their scores when the challenge came from a parent. She demanded I change my policy on grading because she felt the other teachers allowed D's then so should I. I refused until I was told by my principal that I had to because the district's grading policy stated that 60% to 70% was a passing grade. The saddest part of this story was the lady's student was passing with a 76%!

Right after I was forced to announce D's were passing, home-work started to phase out and grades started to spiral downward. I was upset and fairly annoyed. Imagine if the pilot came on as you ready to take off, "Folks, this is Captain Williams and we are getting ready to take off. I felt you should know I am a cer-tified pilot, passing my finals with a 62%!" Does that inspire confidence? In my military career, 90% wasn't good enough. In fact, in many cases anything less than 100% effort could well get someone killed. I still have a hard time with parents or students or even policies that tell us mediocrity is acceptable.

Honor

It's been said we put our money in what we value. That is a tragedy if you see how much those who serve us earn for a living, compared to those who entertain us. Soldiers, police offi-cers, firefighters, and teachers all earn considerably less but have the greatest amount of culpability, responsibility, and training. The more responsible you are in society, the more training you must have—and the less money and fewer benefits you reap from such endeavors.

I remember a talk our flight sergeant gave us many years ago before going to work. The talk was about what we honor. He was a quiet, tall, thin man, a Vietnam and Cold War veteran. We were in Germany getting ready to go to our duty positions, and he asked us, what did we honor? His Jamaican accent was always pleasant to hear, and he always ended the statements with "young man!" One of the guys raised a hand and said, "Country." The flight sergeant looked at him and said, "Of course you do, but that's not enough." Several others added, "God, our berets, fathers, and mothers" and his answer was the same, "Of course you do, but it still won't be enough."

"You must honor our way of life, your family, everything you hold dear," he said. "But this honor must be shown, and there is a sacrifice for it."

We were quiet as we listened to him speak of his story of coming from Jamaica, becoming a citizen, and then serving in Vietnam. He never spoke about his tour, but about the return and feeling the honor of having "served." It didn't matter how he was treated—it didn't reduce the honor. At that moment I believe I learned the word honor can be applied many ways, but only counts for one: service.

Truth

Truth is perhaps an odd subject to consider, but it is one that needs serious discussion.

I have seen my share of scandals in the military. They were, in almost every single instance, dealt with in a fair and severe manner. I should also mention that during my time in the military, many things civilians could do, while in bad taste or perhaps unethical, would be against the Uniformed Military Code of Justice, meaning they were against the law. Adultery, being drunk on duty, sleeping on post, and showing cowardice in front of the enemy, among others, were laws a civilian would not have known about and perhaps not understood. Anything that could affect military cohesion and unit effectiveness was to be considered of great importance to leaders.

However, I have noticed a distinct lessening of such standards of behavior. What was unacceptable in my previous life was now allowed almost openly. While some things may not be illegal, many issues would easily be declared unethical publicly, but winked at by some if mentioned in whispers.

Hard Work

"You are hurting my daughter's self-esteem, Mr. Combs!" The woman was red-faced, angry, and spoke mostly through her clenched teeth. "You told her you expected her to finish this work, but it was too hard for her and now she is upset. What are you going to do about it?"

I had been trying to motivate a young lady to get all her work in. I had seen her do some of the work quite well, but she seemed unmotivated to get it all finished.

"Well, I am certainly not going to let her get away without learning," I said, trying to initially measure my words with her mother. "She is very smart and can do the work," I started to say, but Mom interrupted.

"Then just give the rest to her!" she said. "Hasn't she done enough? What do you expect?"

I couldn't hold it in.

"I expect perfection, in hopes I get near-perfect. I expect the galaxy in hopes of getting the moon. This isn't about her self-esteem; it is about hard work, and she shies away from it too easily. When she learns that lesson, then she will understand and have true self-esteem."

Mom couldn't take any more of my comments and stormed out to head straight to the principal's office. What she said there,

I couldn't have said any better: "You had better get a handle on Mr. Combs. He expects too much of these children and they can't handle the work. I want my child changed to another teacher!"

When my boss tried to answer her, she added, "I expect the best from this school and had better get it!"

It was with great pride, I may say, that he looked her in the eye and answered. "You did get it, and now our best isn't good enough to give your daughter a mediocre education. That's not what we do and not what we are about."

It has been said that hard work is its own reward, and that it teaches self-reliance, tenacity, and the wherewithal to achieve. You can't give anyone self-esteem; it must be earned and fought for. Many teachers try to teach their students this life lesson but are often thwarted by the incessant efforts of parents who want everything given to their child.

We also have a philosophical conundrum—perhaps we shouldn't be teaching such values to students. Who are we to say that one must "earn their stripes" in life? Who are we to maintain the notion that, through hard work and education, you can achieve almost anything? Turn on the TV and you will be inundated with dozens of glaring examples to the contrary. Apparently, if you have looks or an attitude, those attributes can, on a long shot, lead to fame, fortune, and even notoriety.

It's odd to see how the changes in education play upon what we think students could or should be doing. Many things we teach must be practiced in order to master.

Math is a science that sometimes depends on memorization and repetition at a very basic level to allow the student to get better and do harder work. You can't understand trigonometry unless you understand geometry. Fractions and times tables are required knowledge before you can even begin to explore algebra. The same can be said for most educational disciplines. You have to "earn" the knowledge, commit it to your memory, before you can move on to more complicated subjects.

And yet, this concept seems so foreign to many students. Some classic lines from students are quite telling about their level of understanding of hard work and earning your way.

"Well, I did most of the project." I heard this from a student who created a title page and printed off some color images from the Internet for a 10-page semester report. His angry parent then followed with, "He did most of it, and it was in color!"

"Can't I just do extra work?" This student didn't do any of the homework for the past quarter, yet wanted an opportunity for more work. This may come as a shock, but teachers design the lessons, projects, and homework to "reinforce" the learning that should be taking place in the classroom. The plan is designed to help you learn more, so homework should never be given as busy work.

As a final comment, I recall a very odd situation where I had to argue that fair doesn't necessarily mean equal. Students learn at different rates, and this includes all different subjects. Some learn better at different times of the day or are further along in one subject than another.

Sir Ken Robinson makes some excellent points about how we push our kids through in batches on the grand assumption they are all developing at the exact same time. How crazy is that? This assumption means that all of our kids are maturing physically, socially, and psychologically at the same time. It only takes three minutes on any playground to prove that assumption wrong. With this in mind, we need to be able to give harder work to those who can do it, allowing them to challenge themselves academically while being able to help those who need different approaches to learning.

Dedication and Commitment

Great teachers don't give up on their kids, even when their kids give up on class. That aspect alone has saved countless students from failure and worse. Many teachers know the stories from your lives and classrooms about the teacher who was there for their students. An interesting aspect of our profession is that even when I witness very minimally effective teachers (the ones who treat it as a job and follow the contract guidelines as the only requirements for their work), they would often step up when informed of the concerns and troubles of their students. They would step into the role of teacher, mentor, and coach for the benefit of the child. This little touch of dedication can often mean the difference between success and failure for a struggling student.

But even the most well-meaning people can be hammered into mediocrity if the external forces of political correctness, uber-accountability, and the rights of people to stay ignorant are constantly applied. I probably should identify what I mean by those three insufferable elements.

Political correctness: The art of not offending anyone at any time. A dance politicians and teachers do that may subject them to both ridicule and lawsuits if not done perfectly.

Uber-accountability: Putting someone's feet to the fire, especially if they are paid by the government through taxation. Creating rules to "get" people without consideration of the work environment, external stresses, funding, and maniacal policies designed to confuse, slow down, and generally impede real progress.

The rights of people to stay ignorant: If we truly are only here at the taxpayers behest, then let's really do what they want in all circumstances.

Here are a few crazy ideas I think that would help education as a whole:

1. Since education is free, you've got one shot at it. Say you miss nine days of school, unexcused. Why not thank the student for their effort and invite them to try again and start over next year? They would no longer be using taxpayers' materials and resources for that year.

2. If you want highly trained teachers who demonstrate that learning is important in their lives, use that as the tool to reward them. I have been baffled by the calls for removing step promotions or salary increases when teachers get paid for additional degrees.

3. No laws can be passed by any legislature until the two main signers of the bill serve a two-week sentence—sorry, I mean term—in a local Title I school. Or, better yet, what about inviting teachers and administrators to the meetings where these rules are being made?

Of course, I am stating many of these with tongue-in-cheek

sarcasm, but consider the idea that we, as a nation as a whole, and as individual states and communities, do not truly know what we want from our education system. Of course, every student should be in school, but they aren't, and it appears that we are not doing a good job of convincing the populous they should. A disconnection exists between what the politics of the moment may say about education and the wherewithal of communities and parents to live up to those expectations. I sometimes hear administrators exclaim that their community wants a private school at a public school price. Everyone "wants" a good system of education for their kids, but it takes a lot more than funding restructuring or tougher teacher evaluations to create one. This thing we call an education must be worth it to the students, and, through the work and effort, they must come out as better people, ready to take on challenges and able to solve the complex issues of tomorrow. But, too often, we are far too willing to give up easily, especially when the assignment or task is slightly challenging. Granted, if the student doesn't want to be there, you are already fighting an uphill battle. Convincing them that learning is a good thing can be difficult. We need to help them learn that sticking with the work and proving your knowledge is a hard but critical task. I always told my students that self-esteem can only be earned and never given. Self-esteem is when they walk across the stage and receive their diploma, not making concessions on a paper, project, or homework.

We live in a very wasteful society, where computers, phones, and other items are exchanged out when they become slightly used or less desirable. Education should never fit into that category.

Motivation and Leading

Being a teacher is far more than lesson plans and long summers. You must be a leader to your kids. To lead, you must be willing to adapt to new methods, technologies, and standards. So, knowing we need to embrace chances and adapt them into our existing methods is a single step toward creating an inviting classroom. Understanding your students would be the next big step.

We know there are two types of motivation: extrinsic and intrinsic.

Extrinsic motivation is that which is applied from the outside, things we offer in reward to get someone to behave the way we want them to. These rewards come in many forms: money, food, recognition, and other such temporary amenities. And that is the problem with extrinsic motivation: what happens when it runs out? Give a child a piece of candy, and they do something for you. What happens when the bowl is empty? What about those who reward a student for behaving the way they should? Are we sending the signal that you get rewarded for expected behavior?

Intrinsic motivation comes from within. It can be that internal drive of an athlete to compete, or the musician who practices day in and day out to perfect their playing. This type of motivation is far more powerful, but because it comes from inside, it is the most difficult to cultivate, especially when many anti-motivational forces are in play for the student.

The supportive parent who honors education and understands how to have a good educational environment at home will likely have better success of their child in the classroom. But what about the child who's lucky just to get a nutritious meal? What about the child who is lucky to get a bath and a kind word? Many of our children have a difficult time just getting to school, let alone being prepared to help you meet your school's goals of Annual Yearly Progress (AYP) and Value Added measurements.

The Tribe

One key to helping our kids learn to value education is to make it relevant. To make it relevant, you must make it relevant to them! For example, I remember a lesson where I was trying to convey the powerful Medicis of pre-unified Italy of the 1500s. I described how they used trade routes and vigorously defended these routes. How they used the local economy to strengthen both their political and social status. How they were ruthless with control and brooked no competition on their turf. I spoke for quite some time and kept seeing that blank stare in Tiffany's face. She wasn't getting it. I whipped out the medieval map of Italy, showing their zones of occupation and control. Still nothing, but then she raised an eyebrow and her hand, "You mean like the Sopranos, right?" Bingo!

Relevance means making it understandable, making it useful and valuable in their eyes, minds, and lives. When they can attach emotion to the item, it makes an even greater impact on their learning.

Parents

When your values are directly challenged, assaulted even, then there is a good chance you're a public educator dealing with a parent. E. A. Combs

My first big trouble as an educator involved a parent—go figure! I had a parent come in and plop her 14 year old down in the seat in front of my desk and wearily exclaim, "Here's my son—fix him."

I wryly looked up and replied, "Ma'am, I'll try but if I may ask, I get one year with him, he's 14 right now, where have you been the past 13 years?"

That got me a call to the principal's office, where the recurring words of "Mr. Combs, did you say..." were asked. This was a question I would soon get used to hearing.

Parents—Yes, I Went There!

How dare I take a parent to task? I was reminded that in this great triad of public education: students, parents, and educators, only the teacher has the license, and hence the culpability, over his or her actions.

Sure, a student can get detentions for misbehavior, but unless some law is broken—typically one involving attendance or various serious crimes—the parent is off the legal hook in terms of the behavior and education of their child. I'm not accusing parents, mind you; it's just the truth. I must answer for why Johnny doesn't do his work and why he is not motivated to bring in any work. I will be the one to adapt my instruction and change my approach to reach Johnny's academic needs. If I can get a parent to meet me even halfway, it can make a major difference in that child's education.

Hear me, though: I'm not placing blame anywhere, because that is truly a waste of time. What we must recognize is there needs to be a better way to allow parents to keep the authority at home so they can be viably involved in their student's education, maturation, and development.

I understand from my graduate courses that our current system of education is really based on an Industrial-Age model, where parents can drop off kids and go to work.

This is becoming more of an issue as student performance increasingly becomes an element of a teacher's evaluations. I just read an article about how worn out a mom is near the end of the school year. She might be tired of all of the school projects, reading with her children and preparing them for various subjects.

She may, from time to time, just decide to forget about it and take a break. When that happens, how does that affect the teacher, when they are being judged, paid, and allowed to progress based on the actions of someone who simply gives up?

How about a dentist who gets judged on how many cavity-free patients they have, and they get dinged for every cavity seen in their patients? Well, that's simple to deal with: have a hygienist educate the patient and give them the right toothbrush, mouthwash, floss, and toothpaste, right? Do you think this will improve the dental health of their patients? What happens when the patient forgets to brush or simply doesn't develop the habit? What if they don't care?

As a dentist, would you be willing to tie your pay and benefits to your patients' success?

Sometimes I think that a lot of the functions provided by schools become just that: a glorified babysitting gig, and a very cheap one at that. I am reminded of Dr. Gregory's words from Antioch University McGregor: "Folks, we are dealing with three numbers: 15, 30, and 45.

- A 15-year-old pregnant girl, born of a

- 30-year-old mother, and a

- 45-year-old grandmother,

all of whom are quite proud of where they are in life."

It's like teaching a 15-year old girl who has a $300 dollar iPod and $80 jeans about how women have fought for their equal rights in the past. It has no meaning because, to them, they have everything they think they want.

And yet, I have come across so many young girls who think it's cute to have a baby to love them. They think that the definition of self-worth is to have this little being who will be completely dependent upon them. This self-fulfilling prophecy plays out far too often in our schools and communities.

Children...with Children of Their Own

I recently interviewed a new student coming in to the school. She was 14, with her second kid on the way. The first one was already a toddler. Her sad eyes look up at me and asked, "Do I really have to do this? Can't I just go home and be a mom?"

I felt for her, but it also made me think: when that mom grows up and her kids are in school, what expectations will be placed on those children? What standards of conduct will this young mother expect of her children? Is this simply a self-replicating problem, or am I being too harsh in thinking this is a problem at all?

We face this new group of students, and they challenge our very core beliefs about education and life. It can be one of the greatest obstacles we have in teaching: getting students and parents to care. With the myriad of parenting classes offered by social services and schools, we should take a hard look at the evidence of their need, and the rise of the problems poor parenting has inflicted and is inflicting every day on our society.

We also has to be careful not to be too quick to judge the results of such an investigation. It is so convoluted to have a society where 24- to 30-year-old teachers become the surrogate parents of 15- to 18-year-old students. It's assumed that, along with the teaching degree, educators have also somehow become experts at child rearing.

The entrance of parents into the school is often a traumatic time for teachers, especially for those who teach at-risk students. You simply never know what you're going to get. Many times, after talking with some of my parents, I truly wished they wouldn't ever bother contacting me again, most often because they acted just like their child—or worse.

Often they began by defending their child's right to commit acts of indecency and violence. Some of the parents I have talked to or tried to reason with have been outright against the idea of even finishing school; they simply want their child out of their hair for a few hours every day.

The Golden Rule...Revisited

During one such parent-teacher conference I learned of the new Golden Rule. Have you learned it yet? I think you'll be surprised—especially if you think you already know it!

The conversation went something like this:

Parent: "You know, I don't let him get away with anything at home. We follow the Golden Rule!"

Me: "That's wonderful, treating each other with mutual respect is so important in the home."

The same parent, but with a confused look on their face: "Respect? Oh yeah, you gotta respect other people's property! I mean you don't touch mine and I don't touch yours."

Me, now looking confused as well: "Of course, 'do unto others' is a perfect way of demonstrating how to show that respect."

I added a smile.

Parent: "Oh, no, I mean the Golden Rule. You know: 'you smoke your own.'"

I couldn't say anything to match that, so I just nodded and gave the parent a slight smile of disbelief.

The Notorious "Operation SpongeBob"

Another memorable meeting with a student involved broaching the very uncomfortable subject of personal hygiene. The young man in question was so odoriferous, the girls in the class would purposely spray him with perfume. Oddly enough, he liked the attention he was getting and would giggle at the puffs of mists as they floated his way.

The complaints came in, however, and I went into my "time to clean your carcass" routine. The student simply claimed it wasn't anybody's business. When I called the student's home, the guardian repeated the boy's comment. Suddenly, I was left with no other option other than to implement what we would later refer to "Operation SpongeBob."

I contacted my administrator and we made arrangements with the athletic department for the student to take a shower, and we even would wash his clothes. We had a set of sweats for him to wear while the clothes were being washed. The fateful day came, and I instructed the student to report to the athletic department for a shower. He refused, and I called the guardians once again. The uproar from the guardian went straight to the principal, who had to also let the parent know that this behavior could not be tolerated, and it was a danger to all involved. The guardian simply walked out, taking his unwashed charge with him.

Types of Parents

I have dealt with the gamut of parental types in my short career, from the overbearing and demanding to the reclusive and absent. Several archetypes of parents come to mind:

Caught Up in the Minutiae

Because we answer to the voting populous and we care for their most precious commodity, parents certainly have a right to demand a good education and a caring environment for the students. That being said, I rarely deal with those kinds of complaints or issues.

Most of the time, the minutiae tends to be a major focus. And in all honesty, I've never been treated worse by any human than by the parents of some of my students. This is saying a lot. In the military, you can meet some very abusive people. I have often become disheartened at the lack of civility and basic decency some of our teachers must endure from some parents while trying to teach their kids.

I remember one parent who was so fixated on her child's story that she refused to see anything else, including the blatant truth. She came into the office one day, demanding to see a principal. When she spoke to me, she continually used the same phrase over and over: "Mr. Combs, you will ensure that my child is not touched in this school."

I tried to tell her that this was impossible in a building of over

1,700 kids in kindergarten to third grade, but she simply looked at me and repeated the same words over again: "Mr. Combs, you will ensure that my child is not touched in this school. If you don't, I will be forced to home school her."

That was not really much of a threat, considering I had an overcrowded school. I handed her the appropriate paperwork for homeschooling, and she promptly left. When I called the board of education to give them a heads up on the situation, the administrators told me they had already dealt with her on several occasions and were not surprised to hear the report.

I never did hear from that lady again, but the child stayed in school. I do confess, she was, on occasion, touched by other students.

Scared of their Own Children

Sometimes I think parents can become scared that their children may become more or less independent of them.

Many times, I've seen a parent try to hold back a child, and it seemed to me that the parent was purposely preventing the child from reaching their potential. I've seen smothering, helicopter parents, who refuse to allow their child to explore their world and test boundaries, and I've seen parents who see only the limited scope of their life for their child without realizing the true potential inside them. In either case, these parents are holding back their children, shackling them to their own lives of less, and preventing the child from becoming who they could be or reaching their full potential. On many occasions in my career I would have to fight off the depression brought on as a parent left my office and I finally understood the sheer number of problems their child might be dealing with on a daily basis.

A License to Abuse

It's amazing to see how some parents believe that, because they are the voting populous and because they're angry or upset, they have every right to abuse your staff and even sometimes other students when they come into the building. It's almost as if no one has taught them how to stop and think before speaking.

I'm here to tell you that some of the verbal abuse and foul language occurring in our schools on a daily basis is beyond appalling. I remember trying to remind one parent that the use of their language was not only inappropriate and detrimental to my staff, but we were in a school, where children can hear them. She looked at me, said, "Whatever," and continued with her tirade, hurling verbal abuses until I threatened to call the police.

I've heard language worse than any training instructor, used against teachers and me, all in the name of "I'm angry and I'm taking it out on you." Strangely, some administrators seem to think it is their job to take abuse. Some administrators allow this level of abuse because somehow they think educators deserve it—they must think that, by virtue of our supposed lowly status and station, we need to be put in our places.

Classic Parent Lines

Parents and guardians use so many reasons to validate their right to speak abusively to teachers, counselors, and principals. I've heard the following reasons myself:

"My son does not lie. I taught him that lying is a sin and

he does not lie. The rest of those students are lying!'

Me: "I can see you've placed a high priority on the truth, Mrs. Smith. And that is admirable, but one of my teachers also heard your son."

"She's lying too! They all lie here, it's a public school!" — Parent of a 6 year old, who later confessed to lying.

"I don't care what other parents are doing, I will not allow you."

"I hate this school! And the teachers and staff here are rude. I called four times, and each time your secretary was rude and told me I had the wrong number. You are not fooling anyone and certainly can't hide from me!" — Parent who had, in fact, called the wrong number four times.

"I want to know why my child didn't get breakfast this morning! What kind of place are you running when you deny a seven-year-old girl a decent breakfast?" — Parent who called about a lack of breakfast on a late arrival day—students arrived at school that day late due to inclement weather. Her child was home until 10:30 a.m., arrived at school at 11:00 a.m., and had lunch at 11:20 a.m.

"I just received a call from the school that my children are not at school. They got on the bus this morning and now you tell me they aren't there? How incompetent are you people? I am going to have your license, mister! I am calling my lawyer right now. Find my children!" — I immediately put the school in lockdown and had the building searched for the two missing students. The teacher said they did not come to class. I called transportation to find the children did not get on the bus. I called the parent back. Turned out the kids were in the basement, playing hooky.

"I'm mad and I hate this f*cking school!" — Parent told by police to have their child in school or go to court.

"Mr. Combs, I demand that you punish this other child, who has been bullying my Tommy. All Tommy did was push him down a couple of times, and that boy punched my boy in the face."

Me: "Well, he did punch him in an effort to get Tommy off him."

"It doesn't matter. It gave him a bloody nose, and Tommy will have a bruise there! A boy shouldn't have to put up with this behavior in the third grade."

I told her I agreed and that our first grader shouldn't have to punch our third graders to get them off of them. I tried to explain that it looked like a quid pro quo scenario. She then got up, stormed out, and went to the board office to complain that I cursed at her.

"You people have sent me notice after notice." — Parent of a student who missed 86 days of school.

When we give our kids "everything," then they have earned nothing. The idea of working for something seems to be slipping away as an admirable trait.

The advent of ninth place ribbons and "participation" points is watering down incentives and blurring the lines of what is expected and what is demanded. The gym has the unspoken saying of "No pain, no gain," and yet this doesn't seem to apply in the classroom or on our public spaces for the kids.

Shylock is a Bad Parent

Bullying is a big thing these days. In fact, only Common Core and teacher evaluations are probably mentioned more in the media.

But here is an observation that many may intrinsically know but don't openly recognize: most reports of bullying are not about bullying. Also, many bullies out there shake the "bully finger" at their victims—all the while being supported by their parents, who are bullies themselves.

I've had several occasions where I have had the parents of students who started a fight or beat up someone in my office. In many cases all the parents could focus on was what we were going to do about the other child. Even when we had overwhelming and clear evidence of the aggression from their child, their only concern and complaints were that someone else was not getting into trouble for it.

The entire concept of bullying comes with major issues, starting with the right of a person to protect oneself versus taking a stance of complete nonviolence. Bullying needs to have a very specific definition in a school; if it doesn't, and incidents are not judged by that definition, almost every conflict becomes a "bullying" situation.

Zero tolerance as a policy and approach is also problematic; it may protect the victim, but it leaves the "bully" behind in school, labeled as a troublemaker, and with almost no form of redress, or even an opportunity to change their behavior to allow them to come back into the school successfully. Bullying is a complicated subject, and blanket statements, policies, and rules can't address the root problems of it.

The Perfect Child in our Midst

I have, on two specific occasions, been blessed to have a perfect child in my midst—or at least they were so identified by their doting parents. Of course, being in the presence of such greatness made me race to my calendar and circle those wonderful days, to remember them forever.

Right.

One particularly funny situation involved some minutiae of a "he-said-she-said" issue on the playground that was brought to my attention by a very aggressive parent. She sat down in front of me and did not want to have her child in the meeting.

She began by handing me a list. "Mr. Combs, these children have all been lying to their teacher about my child. This is an example of bullying, and I demand that each of these children be punished and be removed from school."

I started to explain that I needed to investigate the allegations and I was told, "You do not need to investigate anything! She does not lie! She has straight A's and you need to act quick before I handle this myself!"

When I tried to call for the student to come to the office so I could speak with her, Mom started ramping up the indignation and stormed out of the office.

The next day I received a note about this perfect child, which included a signature of their local minister about the student's perfect behavior in Sunday school and her Girl Scout pack leader's endorsement. I never heard back from her mother again.

Angry Parents

She's a big third grader; she pushes, shoves, slaps, and smacks other kids around on a regular basis. When caught, she denies anything happened. And, even if she gets a simple talking to, the inevitable call from Mom always turns into an award-winning dramatization of the woes and terrors wrought upon her poor innocent child by our insensitive government institution.

The parent goes on to remind me of her cultural heritage, of which I am not a member. Therefore, I must be motivated by deep-seated hatred for her daughter's race, color, creed, and religion. The volume increases, as do the accusations. At times, honestly, I consider simply ignoring her daughter's taunting of other students and bad behavior, if only to simply avoid the verbal torture sessions from her parent. And it's not always about the shouting; even the calm conversations I have with the parent are filled with snide insults. Sometimes I would rather have a parent spit in my face than hear her harpy tones and quips.

The problem, of course, is that this is the modus operandi of the girl herself. The child learned this misbehavior at home, modeling it after that of her Academy-Award-winning parent. And the misbehavior is further supported and reinforced from home. In cases like this, no amount of correction, training, or advice will do a thing to enlighten the child that her behavior is unacceptable. She can do no wrong and, therefore, no matter what she does, she will always be backed up by Mommy.

Emotional Outbursts to Cripple their Minds and Bodies

The use of drama seems to give a lot of people license to behave any way they want to get what they want. Screaming, vulgar language, interruptions, and other intractable behaviors are telltale signs of some who has been successful in the past and using these methods to get their way.

Getting upset is mostly a choice. Getting angry is also a choice, and a lot of people out there choose to go through life fairly ticked off. The worst thing about these choices is that people also feel justified in behaving that way, as if it is some birthright. (And it may well be for them!)

The biggest mistakes we make as educators are when we attempt to deal with the parents in the middle of their outburst. At this time the parents are at the pinnacle of their anger, incapable of thinking straight. And, in many cases, we allow these moments to rule our school.

I have seen staff running for cover because a certain kid is having a tantrum—not because of the child's behavior, but because of the reputation of their parent or guardian. I've seen staff bending over backward to accommodate the constant and expected emotional outbursts of a parent.

Not only are these parents unable to make informed and intelligent decisions while they are upset, some people are able to cripple a classroom or an entire school with their behaviors.

We really need to get a handle on allowing these events to occur in our buildings. Why?

1. Allowing it to happen reinforces the behavior

2. Allowing anything to interrupt you classroom undermines your authority in the classroom

3. These interruptions are frustrating to teachers and rob the classroom or school of precious time they need to teach.

Educational leaders would do well to set a precedence with parents and guardians, one that says something like the following:

"We educators are concerned for the welfare and education of every child AND our staff. We, therefore, will not engage in shouting matches or arguments with students or parents because they most often result in no resolution or improvement to the situation." What if that was posted in the office at your school?

Sure, people get upset. We can ask them to take the time to calm down before addressing any issue, but we must also insist that every adult's behavior be an example to our students, and that example must come from all adults present. That specific focus can help protect you and your staff from abuse AND provide a positive outcome for all involved.

Shrike

"Any and all human problems can be solved with the proper amount of explosives," the training sergeant announced.

We were outside on a demolitions training course, and the class was very attentive to the instructor. In just a few minutes, we would be setting up our "shots" and then firing them off.

I was particularly fond of the Shrike Explode/Initiator, a hardwired device that could be used to initiate (set off) a series of explosions at the touch of a few buttons. I got pretty good with my skills, and every time we went out to do a patrol that involved the possibility of demolitions, I would be issued the Shrike. On one occasion, I was grinning and probably letting out a little giggle as the charges went off. During the final evaluations, we turned in our kit, and the training sergeant looked at me with my dangerous little grin, "Okay, Shrike, you don't get to keep this," as he held up the little green box. Thus, the nickname was issued and is with me to this day.

The other meaning of the name came from the same instructor: "A shrike is a small, vicious bird that hangs its victims on barbed wire." This nickname was a huge step up from "Madhobbit," and I must admit I was quite proud of the new moniker.

Several years after I retired, I got a phone call from a buddy who began the conversation with, "How much do you remember about explosives?" I became quiet and rapidly went back through my history to see if I had forgotten some important person I may have pissed off.

"What do you mean?" I asked. My mind started to ask some key questions about my past and wondered why in the world he would ask these questions.

He then went on to explain that a local company needed some people to set off demolitions for an air show. Free admission, front row. I mean: front row seats and explosions? Count me in!

I was really focused on my job a lot of the time, but none so much as when I was handling these devices, partly because the team would need something done and I didn't want to let them down. Also, there isn't a lot of room for mistakes. No "boom" is bad for the operation. An early "boom" would be very bad for me and my team.

When I look for the "boom" in my classroom, I am really looking for those opportunities to create exciting and fun lessons, ones that are unforgettable. Much like training with explosives, we have a limited time to make the biggest and best impact. Sometimes what's needed isn't a big bang, so we must pay attention to the results we need in the end to get the job done. The passion is important to give us the drive to go the extra step to make sure the lesson is done right and that we get the "boom" we need to incite our students' minds and make an impact on their learning.

Bus Time

I could write several books about bus issues alone. Driving a school bus is, without a doubt, the most unforgiving and difficult job I have ever seen anyone do. The abuse from students and parents alone would make most people simply walk away. They would leave the job with joy, knowing that they did not have to suffer another moment of the verbal and physical attacks levied upon them.

But I believe that some of the problems that arise do so when we try to cater to the taxpaying parents instead of focusing on our mission to teach. In some districts, I have seen many instances of bending over backward to allow everyone to get into the busing system—and I get why. The goal is to get these kids into school. But in doing so, we turn a blind eye to some pretty awful and dangerous behaviors. If you have the safest school in the state but the ride to and from school is fraught with fear, anger, and danger, you do not have a safe school.

Bus #36

During the November of the big swine flu (H1N1) scare in 2010, I got a call from transportation: meet Bus #36 immediately for an emergency evacuation. Of course, I started running toward the bus lot, fearing the worst. A bus evacuation is a drill we practice over and over—the goal is to safely and quickly remove the students from the bus via the back emergency door. I got to the bus, cranked open the back door and immediately was struck by the stench.

Now, I can promise you that after five tours in the Middle East, 15 months in Korea, and various deployments to North Africa, I have smelled some unique and horrific smells. But this was the absolute pinnacle of nasty odors.

We got the majority of the students off quickly, and I still saw three sets of legs dangling midway up the left side of the bus— three students were still seated. I called out for the kids to come back to me. They did not move, so I went around to the front of the bus, noticing the bus driver was off to my left, giving one of those "It's all yours, Mr. Principal" looks.

As I entered the bus to see why they were still sitting there, I nearly slipped on the newly "decorated" aisle that stretched down the center of the bus. Steadying myself, I moved up and called out again to the three: "Guys, come on now, let's get off the bus, okay?"

I saw a boy still sitting near the window and an older girl in the aisle. She was covered in vomit, and the boy near the window was equally adorned. I could not yet see the littlest one. The boy finally moved and slowly got off the bus, passing me and walking down the stairs. The third-grade girl in the aisle also slowly got up and moved past me.

As the two older kids shuffled off, I finally saw the tiny kindergärtner. She looked up at me, covered with vomit, crying. Gagging on the overpowering stench, I implored her to follow me off of the bus, "Come on, honey, we'll get you cleaned up." That's when she reached up with her arms and gave me the international sign for "Pick me up," lifting her arms and opening and closing her little fingers as if to say: "I can't move, you have to carry me."

Time to take one for the team.

Attempting to hold her at arm's length, I carried her off the bus. But she was scared, feeling terrible, and apparently needed a hug. She clamped her arms and legs around me and pulled me close. Fully committed, I carried her off the bus and started walking toward the nurse's office. We were almost to the door when she got sick again down the back of my shirt. She cried and said, "Sorry." I told her it was okay.

I remember walking as if I was wounded, making tiny steps down our long hallway to the office. The instant clearing of the hallway told me that everyone else was experiencing the smell as well.

When we finally figured out what happened, the story was that the boy had thrown up on the back of the seat, then the older girl onto the window. The ensuing chain reaction had turned the bus into a vomitorium. When this happened, the littlest one simply got sick on herself, seeing no other unmarked location.

The Swine Flu Strikes Again

Two days later, a boy got on the same bus, put on a paper

surgical mask, proudly announced that his sister had swine flu, and that everyone on the bus would probably get it soon.

The pandemonium that ensued caused the driver to have to pull over several times to calm the students down. I met the bus at school and took the child off. The mask was indeed from his sister, who thought it would be a cool trick to set up her younger brother in such a way. I imagine she was at home, quite satisfied that the prank made it onto the TV that day.

Of course, another third grader with a phone saw to it that her parents were notified. And they, in their love and concern for all of humanity, took it upon themselves to contact the press, police, and medical authorities. I can't be certain, but they may have even gone "above and beyond" and tried to contact the CDC.

The circus that was waiting for me at the school office was of "Barnum and Bailey" proportions. It took quite a while to calm things down. There was even a call to have the kid arrested for inducing panic. That would have shown him!

No Expectations

The first problem with the bus situation in general is that there are really no expectations taught to children when they start riding. We teach them the safety points and evacuation, of course, but we don't practice and demonstrate what behavior we want to see on the bus.

I tried to answer one bus driver when he asked me a very basic question: "How many times do I have to tell first graders to behave on the bus?"

I asked him if he taught them what "behave" looked like. He simply told me: "I am just a driver, not a teacher!"

My response was simple: "Then you shall continue to suffer repeat behaviors, since you misapprehend that they already know how to behave on the big, yellow thing." I got an odd look from him as he closed those flappy doors.

The first mistake we make is assuming students "know" how to behave, as if there is some training academy to prepare the kids to ride the bus, or how to behave in public, or talk to other people, or use the bathroom. If the correct behavior is not taught, modeled, and reinforced, we have zero chance at changing it. If you don't believe me, visit your kids where they live. Not everyone has the same rules, and most definitely not everyone values the same behaviors, regardless if they are in public or private.

Viral Video

Unfortunately, the bus ride is one of the most significant times for misbehavior for students. Recently, a video surfaced of a fifth-grade student yelling, cursing, and taunting a bus aide that was shared on the Internet. The abuse was horrific. The things that boy said—with the encouragement of several other students—were some of the most insulting and hurtful things I've ever heard come out of a human's mouth.

After the video became public, there was an outpouring of support for the teacher's aide, as people all over the country were stunned by the amount of verbal abuse this grandmother had suffered. But the really sad story is most teachers, drivers, and aides were probably not shocked or surprised at all by the insults and hurtful things said by that child. This type of thing happens daily in so many educators' lives. Somehow, this dumping of verbal filth on drivers, aides, and other volunteers who help on the buses has, sadly, become commonplace in most cities and towns.

The second problem is the outrageous sense of entitlement students and parents show when dealing with bus issues. It takes a Herculean effort to get a parent to simply talk about their own child's behavior instead of everyone else's. Perhaps I have had the fortune of simply meeting the parents of the most innocent children in the history of the planet, but I find that highly doubtful.

Parents seem to have a distinct lack of willingness to put the problem into check, to address it and hold the student accountable. And this lack of willingness on our part does a lot of damage now and certainly in their educational future. Sure, some drivers get it wrong; maybe in a few rare cases extenuating circumstances might justify the child's behavior. But rarely have I had a parent tell me, "Mr. Combs, I am so sorry about his behavior. I will be dealing with it at home and I hope we can work together to help my son see how his behavior is disruptive, rude, dangerous."

Actually, I've never had anyone tell me that. Maybe it's just wishful thinking.

Additionally, the bus driver is truly the first ambassador for the school. They have the opportunity to make the student's day start and end with a smile—or a scowl. For some of our kids, the only smiles they see all day long are the ones they see at school. Our drivers need to understand that they can truly set the tone and success for many kids each day. Conversely, they can also help the transition to home with that very same smile and reassuring demeanor.

Without question, a school bus driver has to be one of the most demanding and difficult jobs around. Good training, ensuring they are part of the school team, and maintaining good communications can go a long way to improve the experience of all involved.

Span of Control

For a place that has so many rules that apply "zero levels of tolerance" for behavior, we don't seem to do such a great job with the world of transportation.

A lot of this has to do with span of control, where the students are now behind the only adult in the area, and that adult has to truly focus on other things to get them safely home. When the students leave a 25:1 or 30:1 adult-to-child environment and move to an environment is more like 50:1 or even 65:1 one, they have a lot more opportunities for misbehavior—they are unsupervised and have not been told the expectations of the behavior expected.

To add to the chaos, they have this jaunty, end-of-the-day feeling. "Let them cut loose after the arduous hours studying at school," we tend to think, both as school administrators and parents.

But this little microcosm is not a great place for cutting loose. Misbehavior is unsafe for the students and bus driver—and if behavior becomes too distracting, the bus drive could be dangerous for pedestrians and other drivers on the road. We need to remember that our one and only goal for the bus ride home is to actually get the kids home, safe and sound.

We would do well to teach our kids how to behave while on

buses. I know sounds crazy, but think about it: the bus is really just a large yellow metal box, racing down the highway, filled with kids and giant foam seats.

Adding to this, the only adult in the picture is supposed to be maneuvering the multi-ton vehicle safely through our neighborhoods and finding the right places to stop and drop off.

Allowing the students to jump on to this mode of transportation without some explicit and practiced rules is truly a recipe for disaster. With all this going on, we should not be surprised that a bus load of little ones—who do not know how to behave and have been pent up all day in school—refuse to quietly sit and enjoy the ride home.

I see many teachers and administrators doing a great job of lining the students up, saying goodbye, and walking away from the departing bus with that feeling of "job well done." But the mission isn't really complete until the students get home.

Teaching students the expected behavior is critical in changing the behaviors we see on buses. Combine that with an effort to inform the parents of your goals, and you will help create an atmosphere where these behaviors are understood, expected, and honored. Perhaps we should remind parents that riding the bus is a privilege extended to their children, but bus riding comes with certain rules and that any deviation of these rules would mean removal of those privileges. The fix isn't easy, especially as buses become more and more crowded and the routes get longer and longer, but a set of ground rules would help.

Drama, the Killer of Education

Drama is the bane of many middle and high school teachers. Wouldn't it be great if the students just left all the drama at the door and came into the classroom, ready to learn? I know the touchy-feely crowd tries to enter into the drama, valuing and working through it with each student. While this is an admirable effort, I have never found the time—or the patience—for it.

Drama, Defined and Typified

What do I mean by drama? Let me give you some great examples:

"My mom is dying!" the little redhead exclaimed in Mrs. W's class. It was the reason the student offered for not completing her homework.

"My mom's having surgery this weekend, she could die from it!" was the excuse I got when collecting a vocabulary sheet.

When I was working with a team of ninth-grade teachers to address at-risk students, we always met in the afternoon to discuss our students and curriculum, and on this day we decided to bring our student in to find the best way to help her.

Two of us also had interns, so the six of us sat the student down at the table and Mrs. W, our resident "warm and fuzzy" teacher, began in earnest.

"We understand you're upset and that your mom will be seeing the doctor soon."

The girl sniffed and looked down.

"We want to help you become successful in the classroom," Mrs. W continued. "But we know that sometimes these things can really occupy our minds. Can you tell us what's going on?"

The student looked up. "My mom will have surgery this weekend."

Mrs. C. chimed in, caringly leaning toward the student. "Hon, is this cancer surgery? We really want to help."

"No," the young girl replied, shaking her head. Mustering up all her courage, she gave us the horrible, life-changing prognosis that we were all waiting to hear.

"It's hemorrhoids."

The only person who held it together in that room was my intern, who simply stared down at her papers and started grading.

I had to pathetically excuse myself, repressing the laughter at the situation with tears in my eyes and my red, embarrassed face.

Now, the really sad part of this story was not how a room full of teachers were dragged into a compelling story of woe. It was how this young girl was so anchored to this behavior and story that she was incapable of doing anything else all day. In all honesty, she often looked for reasons to be upset, and when she was upset, it became the reason for not doing her work.

Between covering the world events from 1700 to modern day; teaching concepts of democracy, human migration, and industrial revolutions; and preparing students for high-stakes testing, I am lucky if I get my students through everything the state requires. I don't have time to further complicate matters by putting up with a lengthy discussion about why Sarah dropped her boyfriend and is now after Gina's.

Of course, I hear it now: "That brute! He expects kids today to have discipline and to be responsible for their actions." Well, yes, quite frankly. I have found that the majority of students will rise to this expectation if you set it out to them in the very beginning of your first class. Your responsibility is to be the guide; theirs is to be the learner. This concept can be broached and MUST be set in stone before you can proceed. This concept is your anchor. You can use it as a safety point to return to, like a climber on a multi-pitch climb, using certain points of strength to rely upon.

For example, drama queens and kings will come in armed to the teeth with their deadliest weapon: excuses. Enabled by parents, allowed by leniency, and followed by an endless entourage of sycophants, many students have learned to adapt by excuse.

I remember a particular group of walking "disasters," disguised as students. Whenever they came into the classroom, I was quite intrigued to see what they would come up with next.

But the drama expert has often had years of success in manipulating others, using their situations, feelings, and tears. Indeed, the drama experts are often so caught up in their own dramas that the lack of drama becomes an almost mystical concept.

Dealing with Drama, the Enemy of Instruction

Exploring the students prone to "drama," I have successfully identified several types. Forgive my use of military archetypes to describe how they operate—it's the way my mind thinks:

• The Drama Sniper is well trained and patient, always willing to lie in wait until the perfect single shot, then sits back and watches the action from afar. Taking an insidious approach, these kids are hard to detect. In fact, you'll go half a day interviewing all the players before finally discovering the sniper on the sidelines who really started the action.

• The Drama Machine Gunner, conversely, sprays the classroom with sweeping arcs of drama, hoping to attract all the attention in the room—and leave no one untouched. As long as they have ammo, the drama continues! When dressed down or put on the spot, the machine gunner will go for a quick barrel change and load up with the "pity" ammo, which is often followed up by a parental call (what I call a "resupply") to support their poor, defenseless child. You may see this in the teenage boy who will strip his shirt off before a fight and beat his chest—no kidding, I've seen this happen. Twice. Or, the teen girl who starts to call out everyone else involved so she doesn't do down alone.

The Drama Machine Gunner never has just a single target.

• The Drama Minelayer is more covert, laying their little seeds of destruction in the minds of others until— BOOM—a question or comment sets off a nefarious drama bomb. Unlike the sniper, the minelayer need not be in the room. In fact, they prefer to hear about their exploits later on, long after the attack.

• The Drama Grenadier simply lobs one into a crowd, hoping to get as much collateral damage as possible. They are the ones who loudly announce they are in the room and Elvis is taking autographs! Often not well respected, the grenadier is often recognized by the collective eye roll by the rest of the class whenever they open their mouths to speak.

• The Psychological Warfare Specialist uses misdirection and emotion to pull everyone in the room off target. Seemingly random crying bouts or the telltale "anguished-face-in-the-hands look" indicate much more drama is to come—and much less teaching will occur in this room in the foreseeable future. These specialists are also sworn to their own secrecy and, while being demonstrative that something is in fact terribly wrong, only the most patient and skilled interviewer can ever figure out what it is. They often sport a lower quivering lip, need lots of tissues, and most often appear to go into distress directly before quizzes, tests, and report card days.

• And finally, the Drama Commando (King, Queen, or even Diva) is probably the worst of all to deal with. These masters of drama are adroit at launching themselves into martyrdom at the drop of a hat, all for the sake of becoming the absolute central focus of your classroom. The scary part is that the Drama Commando is actually quite proud of their regal status—and will readily defend their right to die upon their sword, at any time, for all to see. They will often be followed by a willing entourage surrounding them, sycophants or those in training to take up the mantle of "most offended person in the room," should there ever be a vacancy at the top.

Your Counterattack

In the military, to stop any of the above attacks, you must deny the enemy the opportunity, location/terrain, and ammunition/supplies needed to carry out such attacks.

Additionally, it is crucial to convince the enemy that such activity will be very expensive in terms of life, limb, or time. You need to make a concerted effort to prevent such breaches of your security.

Once you allow the insurgents to begin to operate in your area of operation (AO), you'll find it quite difficult to root them out and regain control. The absolute best measure is preventive: deny them opportunity so their operations never begin in the first place. You might call this that fight for their "hearts and minds," a phrase I hear often on CNN.

These "drama" students also seem to have a very high level of built-in, righteous indignation whenever they are put on the spot and challenged for their behavior. You can double that amount for their parent or guardian; they have been indoctrinated on who to blame, how to blame, and what current social issue has the best emotional currency.

I'll never forget the parent who came into the school one day and asked me for her daughter's phone back —our policy was no phones on during the day. She then stated, "My daughter called me and told me you cursed at her. I believe that is very unprofessional, and I'm offended such things go on in this school!"

I then relayed to the parent that we were conducting testing in the building that day, and after confiscating my sixth phone, I had become a bit irritated. I apologized if anything I might have said offended her daughter, and then asked a question of my own: How did her daughter call if we had her phone?

Turns out she had a second phone in her purse! Once that bit of information was out of the bag, I felt it only natural to warn the righteous parent that if she was offended by bad language—I had said "damn," as in, "I wish these damn phones would stay at home," then she ought not to look at her daughter's text messages. The conversation abruptly ended there.

What's a Teacher to Do?

Of course, a solid set of rules of engagement for the classroom is critical. A simple, easily understood set of ground rules will go a long way in setting the proper environment for your room. Posted in a prominent location, a rule can be rapidly pointed out by a teacher, who announces the violation and gets right back to teaching, hopefully with as little disruption as possible.

Another critical aspect in diffusing dramatic situations is to understand the motivation behind the drama: it's all about the garnering of attention. I mentioned denying them terrain, time, and ammo. Well, a good set of classroom rules will deny them the time.

Drama is a social exercise, fed by emotion and lack of self-control. If I were to look at any of the above "drama" students, I'd tell you the one thing you can do to make them ineffective on the battlefield is to disarm them. Quickly, with strength and conviction. Simply remind the student where they are and why they are there.

As simple as it sounds, I have turned a screaming ball of angst into a quiet, reflective kid by asking one simple question, phrasing it in a positive manner, "Hey, what do your grades look like?"

It takes the ammo right out of their weapon when I do that. Suddenly, even if for just a second, the student is forced to look at the single best measure of why they are present and how they are doing at school: their grade. Here's your chance to shift the focus of their emotion back into themselves.

Four Effective Diffusers

Rick Dahlgren has come up with another unique and effective method of disengagement of the drama kid. He calls them "diffusers." They are quick interjections, used to recognize the statement of the student, acknowledge it without judgment, and then send the signal that teaching is still going on. The diffusers are almost completely impersonal and said in a very "matter-of-fact" manner. Rick uses:

"Probably so,"

"Nevertheless,"

"I understand," and

"I'm sorry."

I've also added the following phrases to my regular drama-diffusing repertoire:

"I believe you,"

"Could be," and

"Wow, interesting!"

Without regard to the words, the key is to immediately return to teaching. In fact, if you don't skip a single beat when doing this, you'll see the best results. The flow is important—you must convey to the student that you have heard them, recognize they had a comment or issue important to them, but they are going to be unsuccessful at derailing the classroom or thwarting you in your efforts to teach.

The best one I have heard to date is when a student interjects, "This sucks," and the comeback is a cool smile and "Wait! It gets better."

In martial arts, I learned a great phrase to repeat to myself before I taught any class. In fact, they had it put in our instructor books on the very front: "This is the most important class I will ever teach." We were to read it to ourselves before every class. The same could be said for your class. Using a diffuser sends a very powerful signal: I hear you, but we're learning right now!

Many drama specialists play upon an emotional element when they interrupt: our tendency to take offense. You spend hours upon hours crafting an engaging, standards-based lesson that will differentiate to all learners and accommodate all the IEPs in your class. But then, as you prepare to teach your latest masterpiece, some teenage girl comes in and slices it into little pieces with a petty and noisy issue that you will be forced to deal with by interrupting class and possibly losing your cool.

Because teaching touches our hearts so deeply, we teachers have a hard time not taking offense at such things. The key to overcoming the drama, however, is to not take it personally. But remember, these students are just kids. Rarely do they get up in the morning and set about to ruin your plans for teaching the class. Remembering this will help us minimize the hurt we feel when things go awry in class.

Actual Personal Tragedy

But sometimes the drama is all too real. What if it's an actual personal tragedy the student is trying to grapple with? My answer is one I learned from a student a few years ago.

Her name was Meagan. When her slight frame came into my room, she was accompanied by her parents, who quietly announced that she was dying of cancer and she would not survive the school year.

As we sat down to figure out her plan for the year, she told me that while she loved history, it came hard for her. All she wanted was some extra help, but she emphatically told me that I was not to give her an undeserved better grade. When I asked her what her goal was, why she was going to school at such a time, she told me, "I want to be like the rest of the kids. I want to pass your class, Mr. Combs." Her goal was to pass the class even though it was very unlikely she would make it through the entire school year.

I was shocked and a bit unnerved to have this little fireball in my room. She weighed around 90 pounds but, from day one, was in my class, ready to learn. When she took chemo, she would still come in, looking ghostly and moving quite a bit slower, but she still was determined to be there. When the cancer became more severe, she would email me each day, getting the notes for the lesson. Through emails, notebooks, and phone calls, she worked very hard indeed, and she passed the class with a B.

She passed away that May. Before she left us, I'll never forget her most empowering words to me, "Mr. Combs, the next time a kid comes up and says they didn't do their homework, ask them why not. Even if it's cancer, it's still no excuse."

Meagan's will to learn carried so much power that it was impossible to argue with it. She wanted to learn, and I couldn't deny her that. Why? Because it is the power of a young mind wanting its inherent right in a democracy: to learn. That girl had more of the spark of living and learning than any person I have ever met. This taught me that every child has this spark and desire to learn, but it is very hard sometimes to light that fire.

To overcome obstacles is our lineage, our heritage as a nation, but we've all but forgotten it. Kids are resilient, even when they've had a rough start with little or no parenting or protection. They need an anchor in this life, however, and Meagan's was to finish this class. It was a goal to her, and I dare say so often students come into high school with no vision other than what's going to happen today at the lunch table.

This leads me to speculate upon an underlying factor of why students are so caught up in drama: I think that, beyond the immaturity and attention seeking, kids seem to be truly searching for something to fulfill them. They are constantly looking for something to occupy some important space inside them. Maybe there's something they're not getting at home, online, or on their text messages, so they choose to act out to garner some type of reaction from the external world. And because they don't get this fulfillment at home, many kids are looking for rules and someone who will care enough to give them a framework, a scaffold of support to work within.

Successful teachers, I invariably find, have a system in place to set expectations right in front of the students. These teachers are also adept at ensuring the single message of "what I am teaching right now is the most important thing going on in this building—and in your life." These successful teachers work their magic and envelop their students in differentiated instruction, real-time feedback, and assessment. And, they hold the kids accountable for learning. Perhaps most important of all, these teachers do not take a young person's challenge personally.

Emotional Learning is Important—Drama is Not

Many kids learn well when they can feel strongly about the subject. Those feelings help create a point of value for the student and can make the lesson more relevant.

I had once tried teaching a lesson on the suffragettes in Europe to ninth graders, and it did not go well at all. Trying to teach teenage girls about a time when women had no rights whatsoever is nearly impossible. They own their worlds now, and cannot conceive why it is important to learn of a time when they were fighting for basic rights. It seems alien to them.

One day, I put a sign on my door stating "MEN'S CLUB." I met the students at the door and high-fived all the boys as they came in. I made sure to greet each of them with a "What's up, man? Did you see the game last night?" and other such banter.

As soon as a girl tried to enter, I blocked the door and sneered at them. "Where do you think you are going, missy?"

They were shocked. I actually left the girls in the hall and closed the door. We put on some music in the classroom and the guys were eating it up.

Finally, there was a loud knocking on my door—incredibly, I had an at-risk ninth grade girl banging on the classroom door to get in!

I opened the door and through clenched teeth I said, "What?"

One of my girls retorted, with her hands on her hips: "Mr. Combs, we are supposed to be in class. We will get a detention if you leave us out here." I think she almost stamped her foot.

I looked at all of them and said, "All right, you girls can sit in the back of the classroom, but ONLY if you can keep quiet."

The incredulous girls filed in and sat down forcefully, each with her arms crossed. I started teaching the lesson and purposefully ignored the girls trying to participate. It became even more interesting when even the boys started standing up for them.

When one girl raised her hand, I actually stated in a mocking tone, "Hold on, guys, let's see what the little lady has to say." I could see the indignation in her face, and that was when I really started the lesson. I paired them up, boy and girl, and asked them to write out what they were feeling when this was going on in the classroom.

Then, when I started teaching about Emmeline Pankhurst and the other women to have led the way for women's rights, they were all engaged and ready to hear about it.

A lot of what we are told is important to teach—like what will be on high stakes tests—isn't very interesting. Nor is it at all relevant to many kids. If we can find ways to engage those emotions so they can see that what we are teaching has a point, we just might have a fighting chance.

Reignite Your Passion

The first thing every teacher should do is remind themselves why they became a teacher in the first place. That has to be a mantra you repeat whenever you need to. It might sound simplistic, but really that's the way of success for many. The basics are often the most important element of any learning system. As an example, repetition has gained a bad reputation for the past few years, but if you think about it, it is a very effective method of learning, especially skills and tasks that involve concrete steps.

Let me give you an example, again from my military experience. There really is no such thing as an advanced shooting course. Most people think that since special operations forces spend so much time on the range, there must be two or more different courses of fire. But we always go back to the basics every single time we shoot, because good shooting fundamentals are key to staying accurate, even in the most stressful scenarios.

Sure, shooting with the off hand, or shooting while moving are different, but the basic skills of shooting, sight alignment, breathing, and stance all remain the same.

Oftentimes, when we perfect the basic techniques of any task, we reach the point of mastery. In the Air Force we called moving back to the basics "re-bluing." We constantly sent troops to Professional Military Education courses (known as PME), where they would go over the fundamentals of leadership, ethics, major Air Force programs, and how organizations behave.

At certain ranks you had to complete PME training before you could go for your next promotion. This effort to bring us all back into the fold from time to time was very valuable and ensured that throughout this huge organization, the leaders and team members all knew what was expected and how to conduct their business. This was the military's way of ensuring that as the troops move up the ranks, they gained experience and leadership skills needed to lead the organization in the future.

A similar corollary would be having a great mentorship program for new teachers. One major difference, however, is that once you go through a single mentorship program, you're pretty much done in the educational field. My experience in becoming a principal was fraught with a lot of weird and strange events, to say in the least. I did have a mentor, and he showed me the forms, laws, and how to do certain things that were codified by policy or rules. But it was impossible for him to show me other things that I would encounter in my time as a principal, and he was quite honest about it. We had no real formal way to prepare for some of the things that would happen. So, while we have programs to initially train a teacher or principal for some parts of the job, we have no real sustained effort to help keep educators focused and prepared for their career.

In fact, unless these individuals seek out their own training for professional development, they can literally put in roots and stay right where they were trained for the rest of their career. I'm not casting blame—the point is that we don't have a systematic method of honing teacher skills.

A lot of variables are in place to prevent us from "re-bluing" our teachers. Time is the first one that comes to mind. Teachers face an ever-increasing impingement on teaching time each year. There's also the cost involved. I remember spending almost twenty thousand dollars to become a principal, and I wasn't really keen on spending a whole lot more money in the next two or three years. I was still paying off that second master's degree for training that I probably should get while I'm at work. For an organization that is designed for the proliferation of knowledge, I'm not so sure we do a great job of providing that knowledge in a good, systematic, and effective way for our teachers. This is especially true when external players constantly introduce changes that affect every fiber of the school district.

The "Gooey" Principle

Shortly after the Gulf War, we arrived at the base that Saddam Hussein had taken over in Kuwait. We encountered literally millions of mines and booby traps, and all sorts of other hazards designed to frustrate and kill us as we tried to convert the location into a forward operating base for our own use. Specifically, almost every single building had booby traps on the doors and around any entrances.

Notwithstanding, we had a lot of things to do to both prepare the forward operating base for use and, at the same time, protect ourselves. We had to paint the floors in many of the buildings because we couldn't find a way to get the bloodstains off—so many tortures and executions had occurred there, the floors had been literally awash with blood. No commercial cleaner was strong enough, so we painted over the blood.

As we continued to prepare the base to receive more forces, we expanded the perimeter and prepared to push on toward our next objective. During this time, we also faced many significant operational challenges, especially SCUD alerts. We would be notified that a SCUD missile had been launched at us from the north. The problem with SCUDs is that they are unguided and notoriously unpredictable, so it was impossible to really know where it would hit.

Another problem that we faced was that, in this desert, almost every single life form was aggressive—and extremely poisonous. We found at least seven different versions of deadly vipers alone. The odd thing was that the worse our conditions and challenges grew, the better we performed. A saying we used to have was, "I love that it sucks here, and I wish it would suck more." The intent was to put into our minds that this place was not going to interfere with what we had to do, no matter how bad the climate, terrain, or atmosphere got. After all, we were so busy we never really had time to complain anyway.

From these days we came up with the idea of the GOI principle: GOI, pronounced "gooey," simply means "Get Over It." To save yourself from the GOI syndrome as an educator, you must properly plan your teaching time, never panic, and not take offense at your students' challenges or slight regard for your efforts. It's not very nice to say to someone or to ourselves, "Get over it," but sometimes we need to understand that not everyone starts their day trying to "get" us.

People who don't understand the GOI principle get stuck in a furrow dug by their own complaints and emotions. While I agree that we have a lot of challenges out there, we have to recognize that challenges are designed to pull you away from what is important so that you have a greater chance of failure. Our mission was important and could not fail, and I suggest that teaching is so important that it also should not fail. The most powerful and most influential people in any organization are the ones who get the job done regardless of the obstacles while staying firm and true to their objectives. They stay focused on what is important.

Teachers need to also rise above all the obstacles thrown in their path, to teach without regard to all the interruptions and barriers that WILL come. Great teachers know that what they do is so important that is has to happen even if the constant funding cuts, increased demands for testing and unusable data, and complaints from an overtaxed populace try to hammer the entire profession into the ground.

Quit Taking it Personal!

Along with GOI, I have another term I use that I heard a couple of years ago: QTIP—Quit Taking it Personal. Both QTIP and GOI come from the same philosophy: know who you are dealing with, understand they will test you, and don't be so ready to take offense.

I know the feeling; you have set your stage and prepared the best possible lesson on Napoleon. I mean, this bad boy is 12 pages long, filled with reflections, as well as probing and prompting questions. You've got technology infused with video clips and interactive media ready. You even have opportunities for remediation and enrichment listed out. This is your baby; this could be your master's thesis! You walk into the classroom, ready to present this masterpiece, and some kid in first period complains of a stomachache and commences to throw up in your garbage can.

Before you know it, Napoleon is running out of Moscow and your room becomes a festival of…well, you can imagine. Some of you don't have to imagine it because a similar scenario has happened to you. In moments like these, it's best to remember GOI and QTIP.

Just Overcome the Obstacles and Move On

I've seen some great examples of teachers overcoming challenging obstacles, especially at the beginning of the school year. The teacher may show up and find their room has been moved, or they are teaching an entirely different subject than planned.

Successful teachers have learned to step up and over the obstacles put in their path. Professionals will always find a way to make the absolute best out of even the worst situation given to them. Conversely, minimalists, those who live and die by a simple contract, will find the workplace just that, a place to spend the minimal number of hours necessary to collect their paycheck.

I once approached a teacher with a question at the end of

the day. I asked her if she had a minute, and she looked at her watch. It was two minutes past 3:30, the official end of contract time. She smiled, shook her head no, and headed out the door. She was an example of a minimalist. I would also suggest that she was not a professional teacher. Teachers like this are very few and far between. The majority of teachers I have encountered have been hard working, dedicated, and passionate about what they do. Some have been worn out by the other constraints of the job but still come ready to get it done, regardless of the constant changes and extra work.

The first two weeks of a new school year are probably the most stressful in the school year. In those first few critical days, the teacher is trying to set up their classroom, establish a positive rapport with their new and returning students, and make sure that their schedule matches everything else going on within the building and in the district. During this time the new teacher must also learn all about her new students, where they come from, which ones will prove to be particularly challenging, and what assets and information they bring into her class.

Your Daily Attack…of Knowledge

Going back to my military roots, I've decided that one way of approaching teaching is to think of it as an assault. Your instruction is your main attack, and anything else that comes along—all of those other events, dramatic issues, and interruptions that pull you off task—are just diversionary tactics. They are like an attempt by the enemy to thwart your efforts. If you let them, these diversionary tactics will demand time, effort, and resources from you, and, most of all, pull you away from your primary mission.

Three things will keep you on task during these diversionary challenges: remind the offender that what you are doing is of supreme importance, acknowledge the person, and then press on with your "attack." And your approach must be nonchalant and nonjudgmental.

Reminding the student that learning will continue—despite their diversionary tactics—does not have to be confrontational, especially if done with the right energy and spirit.

Say some helpful student calls out the ever-popular, "This is stupid!" Many teachers take this as a direct challenge to their proficiency. But this is not so. In fact, most of the time these interruptions have little or nothing at all to do with the teacher. They could be cries for attention, or they simply could be something to entertain the masses. Regardless, you must quickly address this and move on. Ignoring a challenge rarely works—but a direct counterattack never does.

Giving lots of attention to an outburst will often feed it. You must be sure that the incident is not just a ruse to get you off task and onto their drama. Some teachers are quite reliable in their daily trips off target. Students will know in short order what draws you off and how to use either finesse or excitement to divert you.

Giving only one warning is also key, but it can be very hard for most people. It's an important step to establish up front that you will take action directly, quickly, and without judging after the second infraction. "Swift and businesslike" should be your mode of operation. To this end, you can quickly let the class know that there is only one thing important is this room: learning!

Arguing and Negotiating with Students

One pitfall many teachers get trapped in is arguing and negotiating with students. Neither should happen in a well-disciplined class. Now, don't get the idea this is a turn-of-the-century classroom where "the rod" plays an integral part. Class can be very enjoyable, respectful, and effective with everyone respecting and abiding by the rules.

It's a bit like keeping the power and authority in the classroom. Once you allow something to slide, you'll have a very difficult time regaining control. If we allow a little bad behavior, we seem to be giving implicit permission to behave that way.

For example, a great method of keeping your authority in the room is to NEVER allow the principal or dean of students to just come in and snatch a student away. That's playing the old Mom-and-Dad game. This demonstrates to the students that the teacher in the room has no real authority. It tells the students that they aren't really going to be held responsible for their actions until an administrator comes in. One major problem with this scenario is that when the administrator gets there, they didn't witness the act and therefore will have to spend valuable time researching and investigating the whole thing. It's a waste of time for everyone—and a major distraction.

One way to make this work in your favor is confer with your administrators ahead of time and have them agree to keep the power in the classroom. Tell them that they need to wait patiently at the door, waiting for you, the teacher, the focal point of the classroom, to find a convenient stopping place. The teacher then invites the principal into the classroom, and the principal asks, "What would you like me to do?" Bam! Power stays with the teacher. And, after a few tries, when the principal finds out there will be fewer referrals, you'll be a hit with the administration.

Plan Ahead...or Plan to Fail

Like your lesson plan, having a set of well-thought-out instructions and options to use during contingencies will help you adapt to any situation.

I am reminded of the military's "patrol order," established to help a combat team conduct a more successful mission in the field. A patrol order is created backward, starting at the end of a successful mission and working backward to the planning phase and the initial preparation of the patrol. Whether it is a simple plan—beans, bullets, and bodies—or a complicated, multifaceted base defense plan, each patrol order addresses the needs of the team, establishes a list of needed supplies, and creates timelines and coordination to complete the particular mission.

A warning order is a plan used to tell a team that there is a mission coming up and that they must plan for it (via the patrol order).

SMEAC was the acronym used to help plan the patrol leader create their patrol order from the warning order, it stands for:

- SITUATION – What's happening?
- MISSION – What needs to be done?
- EXECUTION – How are we going to do it?

- ADMINISTRATION AND LOGISTICS – Who's responsible, and what do they need to get the job done?

- COMMAND AND SIGNAL – Who do we communicate with? Who needs to know what's going on?

The warning order simply tells us something needs to be done, and who's doing it. A more complex plan must then be developed to ensure all functions are addressed during the mission, the patrol order. So it looks like this...

1. Bad guys need to be hurt.

2. Command develops a warning order to identify who will go out and do the hurting.

3. The patrol order is written by the patrol leader to tell the team and the superiors what they will do, how they will do it, and what is should take to get it done.

Like your lesson plan, you must know what will happen in your classroom and how you will deal with certain events if they occur. At a minimum, you should have a plan to deal with contingencies such as medical emergencies, fire drills, and the like.

So, your curriculum plan is the overall plan to deliver the educational materials to the students. You have curriculum maps to tell you how the information should progress (logically, chronologically, and what supplies may be needed). Then you have your unit and lesson plans, each designated to help the teacher plan to deliver the lessons in an orderly and understandable fashion.

However, these are not the only issues that can occur in the classroom. Do you have a concise and exacting discipline plan? Do you change your instructional pace to match the needs of students? How do you deal with differing learning modes and how do you incorporate differentiation? How and when will you reflect on the effectiveness of a particular lesson? Do you prepare for future change in your lessons? How do you plan for changes like technology updates, student reteaching, and schoolwork makeup?

As a minimum, a teacher should have their:

1. Emergency Plan (This should be in place first.)

    a.   Evacuation Drills

    b.   Shelter In Place

    c.   Active Shooter Drills

    d.   Responding to Natural Disasters

2. Technology Plan

    a.   What technology will be used in the classroom?

    b.   What will you use for a backup? What happens when you lose power?

    c.   How will your technology be maintained and updated?

3. Curriculum Map

    a.   What is taught that year/semester?

    b.   What is the preferred order?

    c.   How will it be assessed?

4. Units and Lesson Plans

    a.   How do you plan to deliver your lessons?

    b.   How will you react to reteaching situations?

    c.   How you will assess in the short term to make

sure the lessons are on track?

5.   Substitute Plans

   a.   Does the substitute have everything they need to know to fill in for you if you are ill or in training?

When you think about it, we have a lot of plans! Most teachers do these in their "spare" time, and certainly as they prepare for the school year. The better your plans, the easier it will be to adapt or change them when the inevitable new "policy" comes down from on high. While it may sound weird that you have to plan in order to adapt well to change, it is really the only way to do it without losing your sanity. Changing a plan is much easier that adapting to change without one!

Students

The reason for our existence can also be our greatest pain. I know teachers have a certain mystique: they are ready to love every kid who comes in the door and they can handle anything. While they do put up with a lot of crazy and incredibly disruptive behaviors, it isn't without effect. I have witnessed teachers going through some very tough scenarios, and they seemed to come out of them strong and unaffected, but deep down I know these circumstances often can take a toll.

Little Monsters

When the massacre at Columbine happened, everyone in the media and elsewhere was quick to try and assign blame, to find something that might make sense. The students were teased, or they were loners, we heard from the media. It is almost as if we wanted to give this horrible massacre a valid reason.

I remember staring at the computer screen in my barrack in Korea, stunned at the atrocity, completely unable to do anything about it. And, like many, I was stunned again after the tragic events that occurred at Sandy Hook Elementary in Newtown, Connecticut, in 2012. I have now come to the conclusion that evil is out there everywhere, willing to strike at our most sacred and least defensible points, all for the sake of itself.

One of the most terrible aspects of this escalating behavior is that every time someone commits such atrocities, the bar is set a little higher—and the future may only bring those trying to "raise the bar" again to garner the fleeting and awful attention their sick minds crave.

Cowardice breeds contempt, and those trying to protect and educate the most vulnerable of our society have to deal with this fearful thing.

Yes, I know the Sandy Hook shooter had mental issues, and I know there are a lot of armchair commandos wanting to offer advice, but the first thing we need to remember is that while we always need to be on our guard, we can't turn our schools into prisons for fear of what evil may or may not do.

How do I define evil? If I had to come up with a definition, I'd say it was a willingness to act against innocents for the sole purpose of making them suffer or making others suffer. Evil sets out to cause anguish and pain in others or to do an atrocious act simply for the pleasure of it. Once evil is born and allowed to fester, we can blame all the guns, religions, or political parties we want, but we won't arrive at any solutions to mitigate, reduce, or prevent these terrible events from taking place in the future.

Now, naming this section "Little Monsters" is to pay honor to those teachers—and some parents—who suffer with some really nasty kids that we never, ever talk about. Like the myopic vision some communities have about teachers, we all have this set of blinders on that immediately reminds us the child is never at fault. The worse the kid gets, the quieter the public seems to get about holding them responsible. The Columbine killers, Harris and Klebold, were not kids—they were monsters. Adam Lanza was a monster. They live among us and when they decide to go off, they choose the weakest and most vulnerable members of our society to attack so they can do the most social damage.

Allowing and enabling our youth to do what they want without boundaries has become a major issue in America. We need to realize that defending the right to do wrong is the worst thing we can do when raising children. They need guidance, not *carte blanche*. Every time we allow our kids to do anything without repercussions, it reinforces their bad behavior and emboldens them to go further. How is it possible that our youth can go so far without our guidance?

The same helpless feeling rushes over me when I see these new trends of "knockout" games, where people are being killed by mindless groups of kids getting their kicks our of hurting others. To me, the most shocking part is the lack of concern for anyone else. These juveniles are showing no regard whatsoever for their fellow citizens. Have we lost so much in America?

We may find it easy to complain and point fingers, but we also need to acknowledge we find it equally hard to deal with some of these kids, especially in the absence of parents. We try to offer them something of value while supporting them, but sometimes the students themselves decide to ignore the advice, even to their own undoing. All kids can learn, but some may refuse to do so even in the best conditions.

Reality Comes Early

She was an emotionally disturbed child of "special abilities," or so they told us. We had already heard the stories of how she had stabbed her mother and threatened to kill their pet at home. She was known to cause absolute chaos in public, and her legend was already established within the school district. All of these stories preceded her entrance into kindergarten.

The behavior continued after she began school. On one occasion, she leaped onto a chair, pointed at her kindergarten teacher and said, "Hey everybody, if we work together we can kill her!"

During a meeting, her mom expressed concern about having this child in her home because she was pregnant and felt that this little girl was a real danger to her family. It took a lot of finagling to get the right people together to get the child placed into the right educational spot, only to find out the intensive school designed to work with emotionally disturbed children had no more spots available.

The only answer? She remained in the class until funding changed or a spot opened up. Now, imagine this classroom with that child still present—even after all of those disruptions and threats—and the new challenges that teacher continued to face on a daily basis. We don't talk about these things because they are not nice and it makes it seem like we can't get the job done. In reality, it is a different scenario altogether.

All Can Learn But Not All Will Choose To

He was a ninth grader who had failed the previous two years at school. He didn't care what you thought and didn't care if you cared. He sat most of the time with his arms crossed and glared at the teacher until the bell rang. He didn't do homework and dared you, his parents, or the principal to make him. He was quick to lash out violently, and he knew how to cut down others with language and looks.

Dan was an angry young man, and his shell was thicker than anything I had ever experienced. He lasted a month in my class before being suspended for…fighting. When he returned the first time, I tried talking with him, but I seemed unable to make any connection. His parents wouldn't return my calls, and eventually he was removed two more times from school. He didn't return after the last suspension.

I later wondered if there was something else I could have done, or the school could have done, to help him. The last time I heard any news on Dan was reading his name as part of a listing on the sheriff's web-page for recently arrested individuals. This time it was more than fighting, although that was the initial cause. He had hurt someone really badly, and now he was in jail.

When you would meet him in class, his eyes sort of smoldered in the back, with anger waiting to leap out. He had shunned counselors and friends, often lashing out at them when they tried to talk with him and calm him down. Now, I am certain no more attempts will be made to reach him. His sad story seemed to write itself.

The Mouths (and Feet) of Babes

He was a first grader that was beyond incorrigible. When he didn't get his way, and I mean immediately, he would begin screaming and striking anyone in his path. His mom would bring him to school, drop him off, and leave. When we called her because he shoved a little girl across the room or stomped on his "friend" at recess, she would start in with her litany of accusations about how we were picking on him because of his race.

One time, he made a nasty struck a little girl in his class, leaving a nasty mark, and decided he would scream at the top of his lungs, disrupting classes for the entire hallways. He screamed for three hours. When my counselor was lifting him up to remove him from another room, I saw his small, angry eyes squint. He pulled back his right leg and delivered a surprisingly strong heel kick to my face.

One odd thing was he almost never had any tears when he cried—and he could turn the crying off instantly, once his demands were met. Mom would show up, picking him up and accusing me of abuse, then cuddle the boy to reassure him. "Don't worry honey, you didn't do anything wrong," she would say to him.

And I remember seeing his little face grin at me as Mom carried him out. He could play anyone, as long as he had Mom convinced. He knew exactly what he was doing.

"You're Gonna Die, Mr. Combs"

I am a "bulldog" kind of teacher. I grab hold of the subject and the student, and attack relentlessly until we get where we need to be. Tenacious is a good description for my approach. In fact, one of my mentors once said, "When Eric goes after Moby Dick in a rowboat, he brings the tartar sauce." This approach isn't necessarily the best for all kids—and as I found out, it could result in threats upon your life!

A mom came in one time to warn me: her child didn't like my approach to teaching. In fact, the student was planning to kill me.

I was fairly new in my teaching career, and I was in decent shape so I wasn't worried about my safety in the least. The girl was not athletic and usually just sat at the back of the classroom, not speaking to anyone. She would doodle and look down at her paper.

While the entire idea was laughable in my mind, the parent was really serious about her daughter's hatred of me. I did try to talk to the student and engage her in the lessons in a milder and gentler voice, but all I got for my trouble was a steely-eyed glare and a slightly snarled expression. She wouldn't talk to the counselors, and the mom ended up homeschooling her.

I later found out I wasn't her only target, and that this behavior had been repeated each year for the past three years. Finally, each year Mom would pull her out of school and home school her or sign her up for online classes.

Cafeteria Duty

These common areas, where students interact with each other in large groups, are interesting to watch. I was in one school where the teachers are assigned lunch duty at a high school cafeteria. They would stand at the periphery each day and, to speed up the imminent departure of the students, they would roll up the large garbage cans and start clearing the tables.

The craziest thing about this was some kids were acting like their teachers were poorly trained waiters and would either deride them or purposefully make a game out of making it more difficult to clear the tables. I remember walking up to a table and simply stating, "Time to clear your table, guys." They looked stunned and stared at each other. The bell rang and they got up to leave, but I told them to have a seat. I then explained what a clean table looks like, and how they might want to go about accomplishing this terribly difficult task. They grumbled and moped, but finally got the table cleaned. Then I realized, the teachers who came before me had tried before, because now I was late for my class.

I realize there are no parental academies for common sense, decency, and expected behaviors, but I really think we should look into investing in some. When I walk into school bathrooms students provide another glaring example of a lack of expected behaviors. The restrooms are often trashed beyond belief, and most students have the attitude that someone else will simply clean it up.

A Rebel Mom Who Raised a Rebel Kid

A sophomore boy was handing out literature describing the plight of the American white male, literature filled with hatred and filth about anyone not of the Aryan race. Apparently, this boy was unaware that Aryans actually came from India, but who was I to disabuse him of this notion?

I confiscated the pamphlets and promptly suspended him from school. Later that day, I got a call from an unknown adult male, demanding the material be returned. I told him the material had been destroyed, and it had no business being on my campus.

He asked me, "What problem do you have with your own kind?"

I told him I was not "of his kind," and he hung up. I figured he'd get mad, so I called our School Resource Officer (SRO) to let him know about the situation. The SRO did some research and discovered that this group was a legitimate group with ties to several white supremacist organizations. The SRO then asked me if I had a firearm, and whether or not I had a Concealed Carry Permit (CCP).

I didn't think it was that big of a deal until more calls started coming into the school, each detailing how I was going to be taught a lesson. I got the CCP and made arrangements with the police for travel to and from work.

Months passed and the boy returned to school. Things remained fairly quiet until he decided to wear his rebel flag shirt to school one day. The shirt was emblazoned with a message suggesting that if you didn't like the shirt, you needed a lesson in history.

Several students complained to me about the shirt and the boy's comments about it. I called him in to let him know that he couldn't wear it to school because it offended others and was disrupting the academic environment.

He said, "Okay," and I figured that things were getting better.

That was, until the next day, when his mom and aunt stormed into my office, screaming about being "rebel girls," and they were raising a "rebel boy." I let them know that information was irrelevant to the scenario, and I was simply trying to maintain a calm and pleasant environment in the school for learning.

They turned up their volume and I turned mine down, smiling and reminding them that if they couldn't act civilly, we would talk later when they were calm and reasonable. This went back and forth. Each time the conversation started, they would get irate and start screaming. At this moment I realized that I have treated better by declared enemies of our country than by some parents and students in the school, a fact that still depresses me from time to time.

I finally told the women that my decision was final, offering to show them the applicable laws that allowed me to make that decision. They stormed out, taking their screams and bantering to the board of education. I never did hear back from them, and the harassing calls from the unidentified male stopped.

Some Interesting Conversations

Monsters come in older packages as well. And when I recount the "interesting" conversations I have had with some of these "monsters" over the years, a few rise to the top as being significantly noteworthy.

I recall one lady who really got under just about everybody's skin. She would be nice as can be one day, and then a screaming, ranting maniac the next. What made her special was how she would find the most insulting and degrading comments, things like "I can't see how you ever were in the military, Mr. Combs.

You have no honor." Or the equally fun, stated to my supervisor, "I don't trust my child to be alone with him. You never know what he would do."

Over the course of my career I've been accused of a lot of things, but this one almost made me go through the roof. The very next day she tried to apologize in a feeble and meek way, almost as if she didn't mean the darts she threw. I told her we were done communicating, and that all the apologies in the world could not take back her accusations. She seemed confused at my response and went about her day.

Months later, I heard her screaming at the principal in similar fashion, making more wild accusations and new and outrageous claims against her and the school. I guess that was just her method of getting attention, but I couldn't help thinking she had some sort of bizarre Münchhausen Syndrome going on. What really disturbed me was the feeling that being treated like this just comes with the territory, and part of our job is to accept, embrace, and expect such abuse. I wonder if this tendency helps to keep our profession under the social/political thumb to keep us humble?

Fortunately, I tend to not live like a victim and feel quite empowered to call these attempts at denigration out individually and publicly. It is NOT okay for someone to curse out someone else just because they feel bad, or angry, or whatever petulant mood they find themselves in. When we are overexposed to barrages of simulated "righteous anger," it tends to either desensitize or mollify us.

A good example of what I mean is:

We all know that person who comes into our lives periodically and causes a response in us of fight, flight, or mockery. You know in your heart what I mean, that person who makes your eyes roll and you say to yourself: "Oh God, not him/her/them again." This person is locked into a constant and perpetual complaining mode, but their complaints have nothing to do with you.

They live in a perpetually wronged world and mention every bad turn ever done to them at every encounter. They are always prepared with some abuse-laden litany of wrongs the district has done them. Perhaps this litany of problems goes back all the way to when they were young.

I would say this person immediately develops a "punch-me" face when they enter the room. You've seen it before in movies—where someone finally just smacks someone because they need it. Not all people react in this way. In fact, some will cower and avoid, while others will do anything they can to rile up the antagonist. Some go to extraordinary ends to quell the pseudo-anger and bend over backward to satisfy this miscreant so they will simply leave at the soonest possible moment.

I remember one such event where the principal just moved the child so that she could get back to real work with the school. When that happens year after year, the parents learn that all they have to do is raise the volume and abuse the staff, and they get their way.

The problem with this is that it has reinforced this person's perception of their own power and approach. They teach us to scurry, grovel, or puff up in reaction to their heightened emotional outbursts. Not only does this wear our teachers down, it is a huge waste of time! This problem is compounded exponentially as these individuals steal time from the rest of the school, aggravate and frustrate staff, and model this behavior for their own and other children.

I have worked with a few teachers and administrators who have stood firm and let the offending person know that this behavior is unacceptable, but these brave individuals are not the majority. It concerns me that the community school becomes some sort of emotional dumping ground for those filled with accusations, limited parental ability, or lack of any self-control.

We often hear of the grand call for reforming schools and education, but I think we need an overhaul of society as a whole, at least in the sense of how we treat one another, and of our expectations for our schools, community, and even country. Is it endemic that those who serve the greater good get the most scrutiny in our country? I often wonder how many teachers, police officers, firefighters, and soldiers have faced the dilemma of serving those who do not share their moral values of character?

The Arrival of Angels

Now, I've rambled on about the monsters, but angels can be seen in our schools as well. These unsung heroes of our buildings are those folks who give of themselves, their time and materials to ensure our kids get the best they have to offer. These include staff, parents, and community members who recognize we all have a part to play in making our schools—and the educational experience of our students—a safe and productive one.

In my elementary assistant principal days, we had a group of retired folks from a local church who truly imbued the very best of our community. We called them the Helping Hands, but many of the kids just called them our school grandpas and grandmas. Each year, they would come out and volunteer, en masse and individually. At the beginning of the year, I would get a whole group of them together, and they would help us receive the students at the beginning of the day and say goodbye at the end. They also volunteered as tutors, and each year they provided a science program from a museum for our third graders. They were involved, organized, and, most of all, caring for our school, kids, and staff members.

We would also visit their church each year for a luncheon and a "state of the school" meeting, where the principals and counselors would share the upcoming year's goals, needs, and the direction of the school. Invariably, the members of Helping Hands would ask what they could do to help. Through the years, they have provided storage sheds, a golf cart (our campus there was huge), and many supplies for our students and staff.

Finally, they would also offer to help on cleanup days, providing materials (paints, cleaner, etc.) and bodies to help us tackle some much-needed projects or to help with the upkeep of the building. This help was really a critical gift to our building, and without them our lives would have been so much harder.

I knew a School Resource Officer (SRO) in Ohio who typified the very best of humanity and sacrifice. He was a no-nonsense sort of guy, but still had a heart for the students. The great thing about this man was his focus on improving the entire school environment by making sure that contact with police was a positive and protective event, not a scary one. He had built a rapport with the students and staff that was filled with trust and respect, even to the point where some of the students began reporting crimes and dangerous incidents to him in confidence. I believe that his presence at our school worked to prevent more problems and accidents than we will ever know.

I worked with an extraordinary gentleman when I was teaching high school who would volunteer and meet our kids at local parks to teach them land navigation skills with a compass and map. We would eventually compete as a school team throughout the state, and this guy would be at each event, helping students brush up on their skills. He would always take the time with the kids and had the patience to make sure they got the skills they needed before going out on their hikes to find objects in the woods.

There is a difference between the helicopter parent (hovering and never letting the child out of their sight) and one who is a true student advocate. Parents who advocate for their child know that the teacher and parent are a team, not adversaries in this job of education.

I remember one such parent in our Delta program; she was very honest with her words and desire for her student. She pulled us aside one day early in the school year and explained their situation. She had her child young, and the father was immediately out of the picture. She couldn't finish high school and had to find work at a local diner. Through long hours of work, taking care of her child, and working toward her GED, she had learned that the value of the education was far more than a paycheck to her. It meant a better life.

Now, her child was in high school, and the parent shared that she wanted the best for her girl—but nothing was to be given, only earned. She wanted her daughter to struggle through school as she had, but with the additional support so that her daughter could learn the hard lessons of life. She fully understood that when a person works hard and achieves their own success, they own it forever.

I am thankful for these, and many other, school angels who selflessly serve in our schools and communities. In this chaotic and constantly changing profession, they are truly the anchors we need to keep grounded and real with our kids.

Why Teachers Teach

So, why would they do it? Why do teachers tackle all of the challenges I've mentioned so far, and a hundred more I haven't?

In this educational world so fraught with abuses, frustrations, and constant changes to the social and political atmosphere, why would anyone do it? For their summers off? Hardly. That may have been a benefit years ago, but to even survive in the career field, let alone excel, you had best be getting your lessons, and your classroom and academic life in order during those times.

Benefits and Motivation

Is there an argument for the great benefits and retirement? Nope, those are eroding as fast as you can say, "Following in GM's footsteps." Of course, those who have gone on and retired deserved it! Misery loves company, and the working public can rest assured that their public teachers are losing just as many benefits and retirement plans as the general public.

I am reminded of the vitriol I heard at one board of education meeting when a citizen complained profusely that the teacher salary was so high, even mentioning one teacher who made over $57,000 a year! Those numbers might be shocking until you learn she was a five-year veteran with two master's degrees, and if she would have had the inclination, she could have started at $75,000 across the street, working for the government with one master's degree. But never mind, she seemed to not mind the darts—she spoke next at the meeting, introducing her students, who had recently won academic success at a statewide science competition.

Perhaps they became teachers because the schoolwork was so easy. Oops, did you know we now teach algebra and geometry concepts in the third grade? In many states, teachers end up six to eight credits shy of a master's degree, just from getting their teaching certification. When you add in the continual education requirements and extra courses, teachers are always learning—and, by the way that is a good thing. Lifelong learners make great teachers!

I will use another military analogy to help describe what I have seen and discovered as the motivating factors of why teachers do the job. What motivates a troop to go through a god-awful course, where they are guaranteed to be abused physically, mentally and emotionally? What about when the only promise of reward will be an extra $85 per month jump in pay, or maybe a couple of extra points toward promotion calculations? Why are there waiting lists for schools that have more than 75% failure rates or washouts? Who in their right minds signs up to starve in the desert, jump out of reasonably safe aircraft, or be hunted down by very aggressive tactical teams—with dogs?

They don't do it for the pay and benefits. Members of the military are motivated by the job, the profession, and the people they work with.

I joined in 1980, when it was still not considered very fashionable or desirable to join up. Many of my superiors were Vietnam-era veterans, and their disdain for their substandard treatment and the lack of respect they experienced in their careers was palpable. After Grenada, things got a lot better. After the first Gulf War, they improved even more.

I have experienced the effects of social change in a career field that is serving the greater good. I have recently been treated with great respect and have had groups and individuals thank me for my "service." With gratitude, I thank them, but I often wonder when was the last time someone thanked a teacher openly and publicly for the sake of being a teacher? "Thank you for your service—to our children." Never heard it, not once.

I am not expecting any thanks— after all, I am being paid, and some would argue too much. In addition, just like the troops, teachers never look for it and, in fact, are often rather shy or embarrassed if it is ever mentioned or brought up.

Could it be that teachers, administrators, aides, bus drivers, and cafeteria workers are doing this for the needs of the community and our kids? Should we not reconsider the treatment and respect this group deserves and receives?

Sacrifice and Determination

Magical and wondrous lessons are being taught in our schools every day. As I travel around the US, meeting more and more wonderful instructors and administrators, I discover more wonderful examples of sacrifice and determination in our teachers. Countless professionals work in very difficult situations, all for the sake and hope of their students learning to become lovers of education and able to learn on their own in this world.

We had a counselor working in the huge primary school where I was an administrator. Ernie was the quintessential counselor; everything he did was for the kids and for the community. He was a staple of our district and had so many contacts and connections that I truly believe he could get almost anything done. From organizing a food pantry on the weekends to helping church groups donate time, materials, and tutors to the school, the man could do anything. His laugh was infectious and the kids gravitated to him because they knew he was genuine and he cared.

Ernie would get riled up and momentarily angry when we kept seeing constant cuts to our staff and programs, but he would immediately bounce back and find other resources and personnel to help fill in the constantly growing gaps in our budget and support programs. He is also the kind of person you could be honest and frank with and be assured he would not pull punches or water down the answers.

On two occasions I saw him work through some very tough scenarios: evidence of child abuse that came to his attention, and personal tragedies that only his closest friends knew about. No other person would know the monumental issues he was dealing with because he knew his smile and confidence were anchors for so many students, parents, and staff. His dedication to the work was like a higher calling, and I am certain that our school would have been hard pressed to ever find someone who could fill half his shoes.

Servant Leaders

Our schools are filled with many servant leaders, who are dedicated to helping the students and staff, regardless of any constraints place upon them. We had an ESL (English as a second language) teacher who worked with so many families, it was almost impossible to keep up with her. She had a tremendous workload and was working with students who spoke six different languages in their homes.

I would meet with her about once a week or so to find everything was already in order, and she needed only cursory help. We had a family from Libya who were devout Muslims and practices Wahhabism, a very strict form of the religion. The father came in one day to demand that we get rid of all music because it was forbidden in his religion; he did not want his child exposed to it.

I was going to speak with him and, in all honesty, I was not planning to be pleasant or accommodating. Instead, Mrs. V asked if she could speak with him first. I knew that the parent did not necessarily speak respectfully to female staff in the first place, but I allowed her to talk with him. Not an hour later, the man asked to see me and apologized, and we made a plan where his son would do something else during music class. Mrs. V's kind spirit and approachable demeanor were legendary in my eyes, as was her humble approach to her job.

The team I first worked with as a teacher was really a dynamic and formidable force, especially when working with at-risk kids. Our team leader, Mrs. Bell, was one of the most organized, level-headed, and intelligent teachers I have ever met. It was great to see her lead our team, and support us as she met with the administration.

Mrs. Wyatt, a Southern belle if there ever was one, was ingenious and innovative with her students. While all the teachers worked very hard, she was always the last out of the building. I did a lesson series with her once, combining social studies and English, and it was one of the best lessons I have ever had the pleasure to take part in. I learned as much as the students learned and probably worked harder on that project than most others in my teaching career.

Mrs. Chadd, our math teacher, was another super-organized woman who had a hero-sized grip on theory, practice, and using data to improve everything we did. Between her and Mrs. Bell, we knew our kids inside and out, and had a plan for each of them to succeed.

Mrs. Chadd and Mrs. Wyatt eventually passed on into administrative roles, and their replacements, Mrs. Beeman and Mr. Ehlinger, were equally superlative educators. Mrs. Beeman was a singular entity as a teacher, intelligent and thought-provoking, and she instilled this desire to learn in all her students.

Mr. Ehlinger was an interactive and fun math teacher who engaged his kids and really liked working with the team. We had a great setup—we had our kids selected from the least successful students of eighth grade, and our principal gave us *carte blanche* to schedule our program as needed. In this particular case, money and funding was our only limited resource.

I saw the greatest achievements of students who really needed it the most while on this team. We teachers trained together, planned together, and taught together. It felt so good, working with a team again, and one with the same mission and goals. At the end of each day, we would have a common planning time. During this time we would make positive phone calls home to parents, discuss students and their issues, and work on projects together. With this group I learned how to plan lessons for cross-curricular activities, saving time and creating greater relevancy in the lessons themselves. Also in this group I learned how hard they all worked.

Our first year was rough, and we weren't even sure it was working. We were a very data-driven group and, by tracking our numbers, saw about a 67% pass rate. Our principal saw our frustration and reminded us that this was 67% of an expected zero, and that was a very good number indeed. We were laser-focused on helping our kids achieve. It was truly because of their influence that I was even considered for the state award.

The shift from working on my own to working with a team really set in my mind the stark differences of support and motivation when working with like-minded teachers. This contrast also highlights the difficulties many teachers experience by working on their own and having to deal with little or no support structure at work. The busier they get, the worse it becomes. The isolation also has the added effect of teachers and buildings duplicating work and failing to share their experiences.

But who better to share a great teaching experience with than one of their own? They know the kids, the community, and, if what they are doing in the classroom is working for that group, we need to make sure that successes are shared with the rest of the staff!

Another point of magic I see with teachers is the extra time they spend with their students. Not just the tutoring, after-school help, or counseling. I mean coaching, showing up to concerts and sports games, science fairs, and other competitions. All of these are forms of "extra-duty" many people would be surprised about.

I know of several districts throughout the US that fully expect the teachers to be team coaches or class advisors as part of their regular job. I am not sure how many other career fields do this, but I am pretty sure they must be in the minority. I have heard from time to time a parent comment that "teachers should want to go to my son's game, or they should want to attend all these events." Some people seem to view attending all of these other events and activities as just part and parcel of the whole teaching gig.

Teaching Excellence

Excellence in teaching is everywhere, but it seems not many outside education are willing to report, recognize, or celebrate it. While I absolutely agree we need significant reform in American education, attempting this reform above the district level is baffling and chaotic. Therefore, instead of focusing on the state-level issues, we should zoom down into the classrooms themselves to find out how teachers and administrators are adapting and innovating with what they offer their students.

I was recently speaking in Bozeman, Montana, and was privileged to visit the local high school and "alternative" school. The assistant principal was energetic, supportive, and very excited to show off his excellent staff.

I met two teachers who were adapting the curriculum to help meet the needs of their students. They had, with the help of one of their husbands, created a unique software program that was fully integrated with the core curriculum and easily modified and tracked by each student. The students were free to select the areas they wanted to focus on for the next week. As proof of their readiness to move on, the students submitted projects and other examples of work to the teachers. The teachers then helped the student adjust the level of rigor or approved the work submitted.

In essence, each student had their own individual learning plan and was actively engaged in developing and tracking their own progress. This approach touched upon a significant issue in at-risk student populations: motivation. These teachers in Bozeman were finding that the students were far more engaged when they had a voice–and a choice—in their learning schedule. They also found that the students actively sought out advice and support when they felt this ownership of their learning. What a magnificent approach!

I remember when working with the Delta team, we addressed issues of working with at-risk students. While rigor was very important, motivation and building relationships were key to helping our kids build that self-reliance and confidence to empower them to do their work. The teacher's job is to teach so that students understand the material, but the student's job is to learn. You will find that the most effective teachers are the ones modeling different modes of intelligences. When that happens, the student has the very best opportunity to discover how they best learn and, in consequence, learn to love it.

When I visit schools around the US, I see common elements that are the exemplars of superior teachers. Keeping standards high, building relationships, and holding the students accountable for learning are critical in building the intellectual capacity of our kids. Excellent teachers stay focused on teaching, and the needs of their students come first in their building or district.

Conversely, the schools where I find the most frustration are the ones tied down by bureaucratic nonsense, ineffective leaders, and teachers who either do not know how to innovate or refuse to do so. The level of frustration in some of these schools is quite alarming. I find teachers focused on trying to meet deadlines, instructing students on good test-taking strategies, and struggling with how to introduce technology while lacking equipment, funds for software, or training for the staff.

Indeed, in one school I visited, they had to drop their multi-year professional development plan of improving differentiation of instruction in order to learn a new evaluation and appraisal system. It seems that, in a bid to hold teachers more accountable, we may have put the brakes on many opportunities for them to improve instruction and chances to extend their students' learning.

As we pile on more and more responsibilities, the time and funding to truly help students learn may ebb away. Yet, like soldiers, airmen, and Marines, many teachers and instructors seem to find a way to overcome these and other obstacles for the sake of their charges.

From house visits and after-school programs, to innovations in obtaining volunteer tutors, I have witnessed several schools becoming quite resourceful in getting as much help and instructional time as possible. In the elementary school where I work, we have a small group of teachers who are dedicated to improving the reading scores and abilities of our youngest students. They volunteer their evenings to visit a local apartment complex to set up a round-robin set of stations, where parents and students can learn new reading activities and games designed to help strengthen their students' skills. While these are often not well attended—we even had food prepared by a local church— they are undaunted in trying.

In a high school I worked with, nontraditional students were offered a unique program that gave them significant chances to learn skills for jobs while going to school. The lead teacher had built strong ties with many community businesses and tirelessly worked at getting kids into programs, where they learned important skills and work ethic—and got credit for doing so. His passion for creating countless opportunities for the kids was recently rewarded with a massive cut in the program and the loss of his own job. Failed levies and an ineffective method of funding schools have made this a reality throughout the US.

So many factors affect school programs that it is almost impossible to get one to even stay semi permanent. Fluctuations in funding, termination of grants, and the mobility of volunteers all come into play when we try to rely on outsiders to help in the process of conforming to new requirements, laws, and edicts passed down from those in power to enact them.

Of Culture and Concern

Having finished the book *I Am Malala: The Girl Who Stood Up for Education and was Shot by the Taliban*, I was struck by the strength and perseverance of this young girl. She held that an education was supremely important to her life and had both social and religious teachings that told her so.

She was an outspoken person who supported the right of every child, especially girls, to be able to make their own choices in life and to have a meaningful education that enables them to make the best decisions. She was right, and she cared deeply about this sacred right. I think we need a Malala to stand up for the right of education in our country.

I would grant that the majority of our country doesn't hold education as anything sacred. Of late, education has been a political tool designed to create rifts in political parties and chaos in our schools. While curriculum is important, the revamping of American education must start with a willingness to explore the idea that an education is still valuable instead of finding fault and creating a system of blame and punishment.

The greatest evaluation system in the world will tell you nothing if the student coming to the school doesn't think it is worth their time. We may be able to formulate the perfect model to teach any and all subjects, but the students and parents must also see this as an important endeavor, one worthy of support. Without this support, I believe any and all changes made to public education are doomed to make insignificant improvements. Worse, these changes may continue to create a system that is meaningless to the community, demoralizing to the educators, and divisive to our country socially and economically.

While I agree that everyone can learn, not all choose to do so. Everyone deserves the chance to pursue a good education.

Bibliography

Covey, Stephen R. The 7 Habits of Highly Effective People: Powerful Lessons in Personal Change. Rosetta Books, 2013. Print.

Kain, Eric. "High Teacher Turnover Rates Are a Big Problem for America's Public Schools." Forbes. N. p., n.d. Web. 25 Apr. 2014.

Payne, Ruby K. A Framework for Understanding Poverty 4th Edition. 4 edition. Highlands, Tex: aha Process, Inc., 2005. Print.

Scholtes, Peter R. The Team Handbook: How to Use Teams to Improve Quality. Madison, WI, USA (P.O. Box 5445, Madison 53705-0445): Oriel Inc, 1988. Print.

Clausewitz, Carl von. On War. CreateSpace Independent Publishing Platform, 2012. Print.

Woodruff, Paul. First Democracy: The Challenge of an Ancient Idea. New York: Oxford University Press, USA, 2006. Print.

Yousafzai, Malala, and Christina Lamb. I Am Malala: The Girl Who Stood Up for Education and Was Shot by the Taliban. 1st Edition. New York, NY: Little, Brown and Company, 2013. Print.

Suggested Reading

Cullen, Dave. Columbine. New York, NY: Twelve, 2010. Print.

Hunt, Thomas C. The Impossible Dream: Education and the Search for Panaceas. New York: Peter Lang International Academic Publishers, 2002. Print.

Payne, Ruby K. A Framework for Understanding Poverty 4th Edition. 4 edition. Highlands, Tex: aha Process, Inc., 2005. Print.

Ravitch, Diane. Reign of Error: The Hoax of the Privatization Movement and the Danger to America's Public Schools. F First Edition edition. New York: Knopf, 2013. Print.

Robinson, Ken, and Lou Aronica. The Element: How Finding Your Passion Changes Everything. Reprint edition. Concordville, Pa.; Norwood, Mass.: Penguin Books, 2009. Print.

About The Author

Eric A. Combs, SMSgt, USAF (Ret.), M.S.Ed., M.Ed., was named Ohio Teacher of the Year in 2006. He is retired from the United States Air Force; during his 20 year career, Sergeant Combs served as Security Forces Superintendent and special tactics instructor. He was the 1992 Non-Commissioned Officer of the Year for USAF in Europe and served as a tactical evaluator and trainer with the British Special Air Service.

Upon retiring, he instructed Air Force Junior ROTC and attended the University of Dayton with the Troops to Teachers to obtain his teaching license. He taught Social Studied in a school within a school program at Fairborn High School called Team Delta. This team was developed to help 9th grade at-risk students adapt to high school life and improve their academic skills. Additionally he has taught courses on economics, government, ancient and modern history. He later became and administrator for both high schools and elementary schools in Ohio.

Mr. Combs has been honored four times in Who's Who among American Teacher's and is an active outdoor instructor for high ropes, climbing, rappelling and survival for several organizations. He was awarded the 2007 Smarter Kids Teaching Excellence Award and is the 2006 Ohio Teacher of the Year. He is on the Teacher Leader National Council for Princeton and is a regular webinar presenter and speaker for Kappa Delta Pi.

He is adjunct professor at Wright State University College of Education and Antioch University McGregor Graduate School of Education. As an educational consultant, Eric trains educators on classroom management, lesson planning, dealing with at-risk students, differentiated instruction, school security and education leadership programs.

Mr. Combs is currently a program developer for the Center for Teacher Effectiveness responsible for course development and instruction. Eric is married with one daughter. He is soon to be a grandfather.